STOLE THIS FROM A HOCKEY CARD

STOLE THIS
FROM A HOCKEY CARD

A Philosophy of Hockey,
Doug Harvey,
Identity and Booze

CHRIS ROBINSON

NIGHTWOOD EDITIONS
ROBERTS CREEK, BC
2005

Published by Nightwood Editions
R.R. #22, 3692 Beach Ave.
Roberts Creek, BC, Canada V0N 2W2
www.nightwoodeditions.com

Edited for the house by Silas White

Printed and bound in Canada

Nightwood Editions acknowledges financial support from the Government of Canada through the Canada Council for the Arts and the Book Publishing Industry Development Program (BPIDP), and from the Province of British Columbia through the British Columbia Arts Council, for its publishing activities.

Canadä

The Canada Council | Le Conseil des Arts
FOR THE ARTS | DU CANADA
SINCE 1957 | DEPUIS 1957

BRITISH
COLUMBIA
ARTS COUNCIL
Supported by the Province of British Columbia

LIBRARY AND ARCHIVES CANADA CATALOGUING IN PUBLICATION

Robinson, Chris, 1967-

Stole this from a hockey card: a philosophy of hockey, Doug Harvey, identity and booze / Chris Robinson.

ISBN 0-88971-207-7 / 978-0-88971-207-7

1. Harvey, Doug, 1924-1989. 2. Hockey players—Canada—Biography. 3. Robinson, Chris, 1967—Childhood and youth. I. Title.

GV848.5.H375R62 2005   796.962'092   C2005-903447-5

For Kelly Neall

I am a scientist, I seek to understand me.
All of my impurities and evils yet unknown.

– Robert Pollard, "I Am a Scientist"

It's all error… there's only error.
There's the heart of the world.
Nobody finds his life. That is life.

– Philip Roth, *I Married a Communist*

LAST MINUTE OF PLAY

A thousand words. The photo said the only one necessary: death. Gone was the full face with chubby cheeks, sloped nose, baby face and crewcut. Now he was a yellow shadow, an emaciated silhouette of what once was. The eyes once focused, determined and alive, cowered fearfully in their sockets, tinged with hopelessness and resignation. You barely felt a shrug. He knew his song was nearing its end.

It was October. He was exhausted. The tubes were draining him away. What was the point? He knew it was over. Why couldn't they just leave him be? He got out of bed, struggled to his feet, and was swallowed by his oversized clothes. He passed a mirror and was startled by his image. As he left the hospital the fall breeze shook his bones and what remained of his flesh. He was meeting his grandkids so he could take them to the Montreal Forum to watch a practice. He was actually allowed to leave this time. No more late-night escapes. No being stopped by security. This was his last chance to show the kids the place where he once reigned. But he was seeking something else, too.

He went back that day to that mausoleum of hope and desire to savour what was, to see, to feel, to breathe the breath of that glory long since gone. He was seeking voices, faces, even violence – anything that might lead him to that doorway back to somewhere, anywhere. He found nothing. He heard the crisp strokes of the skate blades, the screaming tone-deaf symphony of the players' voices, but nothing came from the shadows, just silence.

Greatest defenceman before Orr they said. Fuck Bobby Orr. Stanley Cups, Norris trophies, all-star games, the Rocket, Dickie, Butch, that pigeon-lover Selke and Reardon, the son of a bitch who married the boss's daughter. They all seemed like characters in his imagination now, long-forgotten memories from an old movie. All these so-called achievements meant nothing now. They didn't add up to a damn thing. Maybe they meant nothing then, too. All those goddamn myths: the good of the game, the good old days. Just another racket. They skated around slashing, hitting and punching the shit out of each other, just to put a small black rubber disc inside a net, while thousands of idiots paid money to holler and scream at them. They even rioted because a player wasn't allowed to play! Was that all they had? Did their lives revolve entirely around the fortunes of a bunch of barely educated men playing a child's game? Some called it art, jazz, ballet, but that was just hollow talk to justify their racket. Hockey is a sideshow, a circus full of freaks, watched by freaks. Those cocksucker owners sit back and count their cash. Canada's game my ass. Just another racket. They sucker these kids into their fantasyland, raise them like cattle, and toss them aside when they're done with them. Run by a bunch of pansy teetotallers; what the fuck did Smythe know about beating them in the alleys?

Ah forget it. Jesus Christ. Who was he kidding? If he had a chance to do it over again, he'd do it the same damn way.

What other way can there be? Hockey was the best life in the world. It *is* life.

He's jolted out of his memories by the occasional snap of a camera and a small group of reporters. He never liked reporters. A few years ago they'd befriended him only to write about what a fuck-up he'd become. A few weeks ago a radio report said he'd died. He called them in tears telling them it wasn't so. Vultures.

Still, he liked the attention. He didn't like their ass-kissing comments – they embarrassed him and he never knew how to respond. He just liked the quiet security of knowing that someone knew he existed, that he wasn't alone.

They looked at him differently today; few of them could look him in the eyes. He knew that tomorrow's headlines would emphasize how ill he looked, and yet not one of the cowards would look directly at him.

He introduced his grandkids to the bloodsuckers so he could deflect attention from himself. His voice was slow, soft and jittery. He babbled something about the current team. How Chelios knows where to be without the puck. How Richer's a self-centred slug. Then he noticed that the Forum had suddenly become quiet. He looked on the ice and saw that the entire team had gathered in a circle and were looking in his direction. "If you find that you have problems and your injuries hurt, look over there," he heard Coach Burns say. "That's Doug Harvey, one of the greatest players in the history of the game." Harvey said nothing. There it is again. The same old bullshit. Yeah, look at me boys, see what being the greatest gets ya? Squat. I'm gonna die. You're gonna die.

There ain't no greatest in the dirt. We all die equals.

Harvey told the kids it was time to go. He took one last look around, and then walked out. Practice was over.

It was like a pilgrimage. Every day a flock of people came to visit him. Not just family, friends or teammates, but strangers. Some of them wanted to thank him for once helping them out; others just wanted to say thanks. Jesus, it's like I'm one of them saints or somethin'. But I was just a hockey player.

What he really hated was the look in their eyes. He saw their discomfort, sorrow and sadness. Worst of all he saw their pity.

He tried to make the best of it. Got himself a dog called Son of a Bitch, flirted with the nurses, and went around to all the rooms to introduce himself to the other patients. Sometimes he was even allowed out for dinner with Dickie, Rip, Ross Hutchings or Judge King. When they stopped letting him out and even hired a private security guard to keep him from escaping, he just had parties in his room. Fuck 'em. I'll be damned if I'm gonna go out without some laughs. But in the last weeks, even laughter began to hurt like hell.

The last month was painful. He had no energy, no strength. One day he struggled off the bed to take a piss. Along the way he saw himself in the mirror. He was fading away so fast he quietly asked himself why he was still here. There was no response.

Christmas Eve. 1989. Ursula, the kids and their families came by. Since he'd been admitted a year ago, each of the kids took turns staying with him. Today they were all here. It was all he could do not to cry. After all these years, after all the shit he'd put them through, here they were, smiling, laughing and loving with him. He turned to each of them, asked them if they were okay, and embraced them. He told them he loved them. When he finished, he calmly said, "Listen, it's time to go."

The game was over.

●

"Doug Harvey died penniless after living for years in an abandoned boxcar."

I saw these words on the TV screen near the end of a docu-drama called *Net Worth*. It was primarily about former hockey player Ted Lindsay. Lindsay, along with the captains of each of the National Hockey League's six teams, including Doug Harvey, tried to start a players' association. It failed. Harvey's life went down the drain. I finished another bottle of whatever beer and had flashes of a hobo character from that old film, *Sullivan's Travels* – you know, with ripped clothes, brown paper bag… I foolishly imagined Harvey travelling around the country on trains going wherever they were going. It was alluring, haunting, and most of all, romantic.

May 1998. I'm drunk. It's my birthday. Yippee. It's a special day. There were a lot of special days that year, but this was REALLY special. Not like the other fifteen-beer days, or the two-bottles-of-wine nights. Hell, not even a forty ouncer of rum would do. Tonight's special is a Canadian Club old-fashioned. A pal of mine from Montreal introduced me to them; they're friendly, sweet and potent. After two or three triples, I give up and just drink the CC straight. I sift through a few of the gifts and grab a book I got from my friend Tom. It's called *Canadiens Captains*. I flip through it and see a chapter on Doug Harvey. I turn to the chapter. The first line: "If he is remembered at all by younger fans, it's because of an erroneous footnote in the television movie, *Net Worth* ..."

I read the rest of the chapter and sit there stunned, fascinated and drunk. Aside from being one of the greatest hockey players ever, Harvey, the chapter said, was manic-depressive, an alcoholic and died of cirrhosis of the liver. He was a faulty, fucked-up human being like the rest of us, and that made me feel real good because, let's see, if Harvey died in 1989, he was sixty-five years old. That's not bad. I could drink for at least another decade or so before I'd have to slow it down.

Harvey seemed so different from Beliveau, Orr, Howe and especially those bland, robotic contemporary players like Gretzky, Sakic and Sundin. Harvey came from a time when players had personalities, when their humanity was still mildly visible, when they really did come from the same community as the fans, when they really did seem just like us. I didn't give a damn about Harvey's hockey feats. I read about how he was the greatest defenceman to ever play the game until Orr came along. He was the quarterback of those amazing 1950s Habs teams that won five straight Stanley Cups. And reportedly he could, when he felt like it, control the tempo of a game.

But so what? I was more interested in the man. There was something familiar: the anger, irrationality and moodiness. A classic Dionysian figure, burning through every moment. Harvey looked and acted like he didn't give a damn about anything. If Canadians are supposed to be polite, reserved, gentle and peaceful, Doug Harvey seemed to be almost anti-Canadian. If hockey was rock and roll, Doug Harvey was Jerry Lee Lewis – a talented, tormented, restless and wild soul straddling that edge between good and evil, between sin and salvation. Harvey wasn't hockey's only fuck-up. He may not have even been its wildest, as the self-destructive lives of Brian Spencer, Bryan Fogarty, Bob Probert and John Kordic, among others, testify, but Harvey was one of the few who was any damn good at playing hockey.

And that didn't even begin to tell the whole story. Harvey was no Jerry Lee Lewis. Harvey also possessed sensitivity, gentleness, empathy and had a genuine love of people. Somewhere deep down inside the shadows of his soul, there rested a shy, lonely man who just wanted to be wanted. Drinking broke down the social barriers. On the ice, he played with the cold calm of a scientist. Off the ice, he gave the impression that he didn't give a damn. He was a loose, free-spirited guy who did what he wanted. But that was misleading. He cared more than many might have realized. When Dickie Moore's son died, Harvey was the first one there. When Habs coach Dick Irvin was dying in the hospital, not one player called or visited until Harvey organized it.

When fans were attacking referee Red Storey during a game in Chicago, Harvey was the only player who came to his aid. He gave days and days of support to poor children and never failed to help anyone who needed it. And we're not talking about tossing a coin and moving on; Harvey was the kind of person who not only offered a hard-luck guy some cash, but he'd invite him into his life.

Sometimes it seemed he cared more about others than even himself. But when it came to his own family, he continually fell short. He was rarely home. He blew all his earnings. When he was home, he was often distracted or drunk. He didn't understand it himself. He loved Ursula and the kids. Maybe it was that old line: familiarity breeds contempt. Maybe he hated the man he saw through their eyes.

NO ANNOUNCEMENTS

December 19, 1924, Montreal. There wasn't much happening. Then, as now, people talked about the weather. Cold temperatures were ravaging western Canada and California. The partially frozen body of a young boy was found. The owner of a "disorderly" house swore she gave the Montreal police chief a ten-dollar bribe to leave her place alone. The Pope lashed out against commies and socialists. And Eaton's reminded readers that there was still time to get their Xmas catalogue. The Montreal Canadiens, the defending Stanley Cup champions, were preparing to host the Ottawa Senators the following evening at the Mont Royal Arena.

While all of this was happening Martha Harvey was giving birth to a child – the birth goes unannounced in the papers. Announcements were only for the high society types, and the Harvey family were lower middle class at best. The papers didn't care about the daily life of the lower class unless there was something dark, dirty, scandalous or heroic about it. In time the boy, Doug Harvey, would give them all that and more.

May 22, 1967, Ottawa. Talk of war in the Middle East. Canada was accused of fence sitting over the Vietnam conflict. Three pilots died in a plane crash at the Uplands Air Base. Two hundred people burned to death in a fire in Brussels.

You could head to the Star Top or Auto-Sky drive-in to check out the new Elvis flick, *Spinout*, or the Marty Robbins-led country jamboree, *Road to Nashville*. Then head over to the Alexandria Hotel at Bank and Gilmour for some go-go gals.

Sometime around noon, I popped out. There were no announcements. There was no father.

We were born forty-two years apart. When I was born, Doug Harvey's life was beginning to fall apart.

NO DAMN GOOD

The first settlers arrived in Ville-Marie (Montreal) in 1650. Facing a continual food crisis and under the constant threat of Indian attack, they were forced to find some new land settlements to strengthen their position. A portion of one new settlement, Coteau Saint-Pierre, eventually formed around the Notre-Dame-de-Toutes-Grâce's parish. In 1876, the Village of Notre-Dame-de-Grâce (NDG) was established. In 1910, NDG was annexed to the city of Montreal.

During Harvey's youth, NDG was manic, laced with schizoid tracks of delusion and ecstasy, tranquillity and violence. It was a place where you could court the girl of your dreams or do a drunken dick dance with the first-available, price-is-right whore. NDG had lots of parks, cute kids, good families, but around any corner you might also discover another world of drunks, hobos and havoc.

"It was a small-town atmosphere," notes former NHL official Red Storey, who grew up in NDG. "A lot of hockey players lived in NDG. There were a lot of normal, hard-working people living there. They just didn't have as much money as other communities."

Alfred Harvey met his future wife, Martha, during the darkest of moments, while bringing her dead fiancé's belongings to her. The couple stayed in touch, hormones bloomed, and in 1921 they were married in Kingston,

Ontario. That same year they set up shop in NDG. A year later, their first boy, Alfred Jr., crawled out of the wet darkness.

Throughout the twenties, the Harvey family moved a number of times within the NDG area. Things were tight, so tight that Alfred – who was working for a local Pharmaceuticals company – had to bike to work. The kids, however, never missed a meal. "We never went hungry, but it was close a few times," Doug once said. Alfred and Martha were strict, spiritual and fair. They encouraged and supported their children (along with Alfred and Doug, there were two younger siblings, Howard and Mary), and provided them with a loving home.

Despite its rough patches, NDG was generally a good place for kids. There were lots of parks nearby to keep them – and the many unemployed men of the 1930s – occupied. The Harvey boys had no problem finding a casual game of football or hockey and there were even community hockey and softball leagues in the area. With little else to do, the brothers spent most of their waking hours playing football, baseball or hockey with the locals.

Alfred and Martha supported these athletic endeavours and managed to keep the boys equipped with whatever gear they needed. They always had skates, baseball mitts, football cleats and a football, and if other kids in the area needed something, they knew who to call on.

Harvey's hockey career officially began at age thirteen when a bantam team, in need of some extra players, invited him to strap on the goalie pads. His career as a goaltender was short-lived and he soon moved up to forward. Eventually, he switched to defence: "I liked it better because you got a lot more playing that way – fifty to fifty-five minutes."

Harvey's early hockey performance was unspectacular. He was undisciplined and had a mean temper. He spent more time fighting than skating. "I had a terrible temper when I started out, in fact," Harvey told one interviewer. "But I tried to overcome it." At this stage, he showed little promise as a hockey player.

Cumberland is a small village twenty kilometres from Ottawa. I spent most of my early childhood there. We didn't have a major pro team in Ottawa then – unless you counted the Ottawa Nationals who played one season (1972–73) in the World Hockey Association. I didn't. The Nationals sucked. This didn't stop me: I found hockey anyway. I don't remember how, when, or why, but there it was. In fact, aside from a few fragments of smiles, laughter, faces and, hey, even a little love, all my early memories are connected with hockey.

I don't really remember playing all that much, at least until I was about seven or eight years old. Most of the memories are patchy images from games, books and hockey cards. And who knows how truthful they are? Memory is the best storyteller. Did I really see Henderson's goal in 1972 and Pocket Rocket's Stanley Cup winner against the Hawks in 1973 or have they just tricked their way into an imagined past? Maybe they are the only things I want to remember from my childhood.

Harvey was a troublemaker in and out of school. Much of it stemmed from boredom and curiosity. He wanted to see how far he could bend the world. When he wasn't shooting kids in the head with a BB gun, or knocking the streetcar trolley-wheels off, he was often – without his parents knowing where he was – wandering off to other towns and places.

He wasn't a rebel, he was just a kid who needed constant stimulation. Between school and church, life could be dull and Harvey seemed pretty determined to create his own pleasure. Then again, how much of his mischievous behaviour was connected to his undiagnosed manic depression? Was his constant search for stimulation just a restless mania, where one minute you can jump off a cliff and the next you can't get out of bed?

Mom and I moved to the city when I was two. All of a sudden there was this guy with us. Where'd he come from? Whatever smiles and good feelings I had in Cumberland were now gone, replaced with frustration and anger. By age five, I was telling crossing guards to "get fucked," attempting to drive the car (while Mom ran into the corner store and left it idling), and pushing a girl I really liked into a brick wall. Why was everyone yelling all the time?

At school Harvey did okay when he wanted to, which wasn't often. He was soft-spoken and shy, but generally got along well in class. School bored him. His mind often wandered. School was just a space between sleep and sports.

During his teens, Harvey could play virtually any sport well. At West Hill High School, he excelled in hockey, baseball, football, soccer, lacrosse, track, snooker, boxing and even badminton. Right up to the time he attended his first Montreal Canadiens training camp in 1945, hockey wasn't even a clear-cut first choice; in fact, at the time Harvey was arguably better at football. He was the star player on the West Hill Senior Football team and after he enlisted in 1942, he starred for the Navy in the Quebec Rugby Football Union (a sort of precursor to the Canadian Football League). In 1943, he was named the league's Most Valuable Player. Harvey would have had a Grey Cup ring in 1944, but the Navy had shipped him out (at his request) before the game.

During his Navy time, Harvey attended a boxing show at the barracks. The champion challenged anyone there to a fight. Harvey jumped in the ring and knocked the champ out in the first round.

Harvey spent most of his summers as a teen playing softball. He played for the NDG team and also joined the Snowdon Fastball League. Former Canadiens and Ottawa Senators manager Tommy Gorman was running a baseball team in Ottawa called the Nationals that had just joined the newly formed Border League. Gorman, who knew Harvey, invited him to play in Ottawa, and as baseball didn't clash with hockey, Harvey accepted.

Between 1947 and 1950, Harvey was a star right fielder with the Nationals. During his first Canadiens training camp, in St. Hyacinthe, Quebec, Harvey actually drove back and forth between camp and Ottawa. "We played at night," said Harvey. "So after the game I'd get in my car and drive to St. Hyacinthe. That's about 40 miles from Montreal, so it was about 160 miles one way. After hockey practice the next morning I'd drive back once again for the ball game. I only had to do it for about a week. When you're young, you can do those things, eh?"

In 1949, Harvey led the Border League with a .351 batting average. That same year he was drafted by the Boston Braves (now Atlanta) of the National League and offered a spot with their Class-B team in Pawtucket. Harvey turned down the offer: "I figure baseball was a good sport, but when Boston Braves drafted me I was twenty-two or twenty-three, too old. If they had signed me when I was eighteen or so, then it might have been different. I might have given it a try." Harvey stayed with the Nationals until 1950 when he finally committed himself full-time to the Montreal Canadiens.

"He was an exceptional athlete," remembers Red Storey. "He was the best all-around athlete who played hockey."

●

My mom used to force me to eat asparagus sandwiches. Only recently did it dawn on me that this wasn't even close to being a normal food pairing – unless you're from Romania. Maybe it was revenge? I was a drunken mistake. Beyond that, I don't even remember much about her. Most days she was quiet, lost in some dark space, occasionally spewing venom about something, someone. She was often distracted, never listening to what anyone was saying. In the meantime, not-really-my-pops was rarely around. He worked shifts. Even when he was there, he wasn't there. No one talked. No one listened. Sometimes everyone screamed.

I became an inadvertent troublemaker. I don't think I planned on it. I just didn't know – no surprise – how to socialize. So when I didn't get what I wanted, I hit, slugged, wrestled, screamed, kicked and swore at everyone. Suddenly there were detentions and meetings. "What's wrong with this boy?" My mom always ignored them. The world was messed up, not her boy. It all sounded so heroic, but she was just defending herself, not me. In fact, there *was* something wrong with me. I wanted these two ghosts in the house to become human.

Fortunately there was hockey.

THE PUCK

When you think about it, it's quite ridiculous: a group of young men beating the shit out of each other to possess a little piece of black rubber. Men have sacrificed their bodies, their brains, their youth and their families all in chase of this stupid puck. That these boys are paid millions to pursue this as a career seems even more insane.

No one ever seems to ask, *why* the puck? Why the obsession, the need, the desire to chase this little piece of rubber around and around? What motivates these boys? Certainly it's a way of harnessing aggression in men. Better they chase a puck and clobber each other than run rampant on the streets doing the same to the locals.

Undoubtedly a lot of it was connected with the illusion of what being a *man* meant. In Harvey's era, and even when I was growing up in the 1970s, *men* were the heroes, gods and mythmakers. Women were kitchen-dwellers: they made dinner, did laundry and sewed. Being a man meant displaying aggression and possessing power. The sons played with toy guns and trucks. Silent and subtle was this gender pressure; so subtle there was no way we'd know. We learned from what we saw and we saw that men were cops, firemen, doctors, truck drivers, car drivers, bus drivers and when they weren't, they were hockey players. Women drooled over them. Women fucked them and fawned over them. You're drawn into this world before you even recognize it.

Sport was a male world. It was where we all bonded quietly. Girls didn't get it. They played with dolls. Women could just be, but men, they had to be someone. How many men are still fucked up by these compartments? How many are stuck in prescribed roles for fear that they'll be called pussies?

Hockey, and sport in general, was also an escape from dreary small-town life. If your only options are working in a mine, a factory, or sales, hockey is a pretty damn good alternative. The fathers of Harvey's generation had lived through a horrific war and their reward was a decade of economic depression. When they could work, they worked shitty jobs, jobs they probably hated, but they were jobs they needed to put food on the table. Sport was no different than playing cowboys and Indians. It was a fantasy world where the problems of food, rent and survival vanished. Sport also offered a possible escape. For kids, it was a chance for a better life. For their fathers, it was an opportunity, through their sons, to escape the taxing, mundane grind.

But it wasn't all just rooted in masculinity, poverty and violence. Hockey could also be as beautiful, provocative, creative, intellectual and spontaneous as any poem, painting, song or film. Rocket Richard, Bobby Orr and Gordie Howe are artists in the same vein as the free-jazz improv of Cecil Taylor or Albert Ayler, the spontaneous chaos of Jackson Pollock, or even the cameraless cinematic dances of Norman McLaren. Spontaneity is an integral part of hockey. The games go at such a fast clip that the unexpected is a natural part of the game. In a split second, bodies are forced to react, to shift, dart, freeze and fight. Stuff happens. You're either ready or you're not. You adapt or you don't. The game goes on.

Skating let you cheat. You moved faster with less effort. It was addictive: all the gain, less strain. Whether playing alone or with others, the combination of the breeze, the cold, the rhythm of each skate slash is serene, harmonious and gentle. In the winter of 2003, it often reached minus-thirty degrees Celsius with the wind chill. We'd all bitch about the weather but every Friday night, NO MATTER WHAT, a group of us put on layers of clothing and went skating. Once you made it past the initial bone-chilling cold of the first ten to fifteen minutes, the sweat started to build, the legs warmed and winter vanished. It's hypnotic, like the buzz of alcohol. You never want to lose that feeling, but eventually your back and legs can't do it any more, you've gotta take off the skates, get off the cloud, and walk. Your first steps tease you with the echoed glides of the skates. Then it's gone.

SKATING IN CIRCLES

I grew up in the seventies, a child of the expansion era. I was obsessed with anything remotely related to hockey: street hockey, ice hockey, hockey cards, the Loblaws NHL stamp-book collection, *Hockey Night in Canada* and even the NBC game of the week.

I never played competitive or league hockey. I remember attending Peter Lee's Hockey School for a week and then briefly attending a session that would lead to playing with a team. But I never played. I don't know what happened. I always blamed my mom: she made me choose between swimming and hockey. Ha, water and ice. I chose water. I'll never know why I made that decision. All those goddamn early mornings swimming back and forth in cold water.

I didn't play, but I knew all the players, their stats, and their numbers. I was a Boston Bruins fan. Why? Someone bought me a Bruins jersey. In fact, the first game I most clearly remember was the last game of the Flyers–Bruins final of 1974. I was pissed off that the Flyers won. They reminded me of school bullies and cops. And bullies and cops reminded of me of not-really-my-pops. Not-really-my-pops, like Flyers enforcer Dave Schultz, enjoyed making people look weak and stupid.

Although no one told me until I was fifteen, it turned out this not-really-my-pops came from England. He came over when he was eighteen, a few months after I got squirted from the womb. His father had died when he was young and he came to Canada to get away from his coddling mom. He came to the New World to find his own way, his own life. He'd hoped to be an architect, but when that failed he became a shoe clerk on Sparks Street in downtown Ottawa (where he may have encountered Doug Harvey a few times). Then he met my mom at some hippie party, married her, and got a gig as a cop.

Not-really-my-pops didn't abuse me in the traditional sense. Most of the time it was verbal abuse or an open hand wind-up. He loved to cock that right hand back and then fake a punch or a slap to my head. I wish he'd have hit me more often – at least there would have been some closure. Instead I still see that fist circling round and round like a patrol car. You keep anxiously waiting for something to go down.

I hated the Flyers.

Hockey got me in trouble with everyone. I wanted to possess everything hockey related: I traded a brand new baseball glove for a Ken Dryden card, I used to steal money to get the Loblaws hockey stickers, and I even pulled off a major heist of a neighbour's sports cards. This older boy had the best collection of cards. While he was flirting with his girlfriend,

I ventured over to his house and told his mom and brother that he had asked me to come and fetch his cards for him. They reluctantly handed them over. Of course, I didn't bring them to the boy. Instead, I headed for my room and put them in my closet. The brother ratted me out and soon after both boys came a-calling. Incredibly my mom defended me and I got away with it. It made life in the neighbourhood awkward, though, because I guess word got around about me being this crazy kid. I lost two close friends because their parents wouldn't let me play with them any more. And naturally I had to avoid these two brothers. I guess my desperate obsession to possess every hockey card made the fear evaporate. I *had* to possess those cards.

At age seven, not-really-my-pops told me to pack my things, tossed me in the car, and drove me to the Children's Aid Society. Along the way I was told that I was a bad person and that I'd never see any of my friends or family again. When we got there I was told that the building was closed. Some thirty years later not-really-my-pops claims he was only trying to get my mom to take more responsibility for me. She was still angry at bio-pops and was content to just ignore me forever. They apparently reached an agreement to put me up for adoption. But not-really-my-pops wasn't really going to do it. He was just trying to scare the crap out of her. He says he never really imagined it would have hurt me.

Hockey made all the pain and hurt that I didn't really comprehend at the time go away. When I was on the neighbourhood rink or road, I didn't need to talk, I didn't need to smile or find the right words. I just had to score or make a save or stop the other guys, just like they did on TV.

At home, hockey cards let me escape the fear and darkness. I made up all sorts of games with the cards that let me lose myself in a place where no one yelled or screamed, where I wasn't a "useless idiot," where I could pretend that I mattered. We had those traditional street games where you tried to land cards closest to the curb, but I preferred recreating games by lining up my teams on the rug in my room. I used the nets and puck from a table hockey game and had games of my own. It was pretty limited, so I soon turned to playing whole seasons out using dice. I'd "play" a full season by using an existing NHL schedule and rolling the dice to determine the outcome of each game. In this world I was God.

Harvey had no idea at the time that he was manic-depressive, but he must have wondered why he would feel so high one moment and so down the next. He was a shy guy, not the most articulate person, and not the most socially skilled. Sport was an escape for him, but it also provided a balance. It was a forum where he quickly became successful. And with success came social ease. He didn't need to talk. Sport was communal. He spoke through his plays. He earned respect for his skill.

Sport wasn't about becoming someone else for Doug Harvey; it was about finding a comfort zone for the self that existed, about creating a space where he could control the moods and social fears. Here was a space where he was accepted, where he was successful, where all those dark demons left him alone. But his addiction to sport made life even more difficult in the end because he couldn't stay on the ice forever. At some point, he had to leave the rink.

In different ways, hockey let me, Harvey, and thousands upon thousands of boys put off growing up. Unfortunately, this often came at the cost of a formal education: and yeah, okay, is it better to know Dante or to be able to fix a car or a water pipe? I don't know. What many of these boys, especially of the pre-Gretzky era, failed to see was that hockey was little more than a whisper of life's breath. The lack of education, immaturity and the naive desire to play at any price left these guys ripe for exploitation by the owners and managers.

"We were led by a string," says Harvey's old Canadiens teammate, Dickie Moore. "We needed teachers but we never learned anything because it was all done for us. I didn't like it. I wanted some knowledge. We weren't taught anything about life or how to work. You had to pick it up yourself. That's the way it was run. They didn't want to educate us."

But when their careers ended (and for some it was abrupt), they were fucked. Suddenly you're twenty-five, thirty, or thirty-five years old, out of work, and don't know who you are any more. They thought the game was gonna go on forever. A few manage to stay on the island as coaches, managers, broadcasters but most are not so lucky. Every year there are hundreds of Dantes lost in the woods of sports. Doug Harvey would be one of them.

For the most part, I was just like other kids. I was aggressive. I had lots of energy to unleash and sports and fighting were ideal outlets. But as my home life generated even more anger and violence in me, hockey became a means to salvation, one that I desperately needed in order to feel sane. So why didn't the hockey-mad boy ever play organized ice hockey? Well, if I had, I may have very quickly realized that I wasn't a good enough player. Then I'd have nothing. By avoiding league hockey I ensured that the illusion would survive and flourish. There was always hope. There was always a possibility. Maybe I didn't even want to be a hockey player; maybe I just wanted to be somebody else. I was no more than seven fucking years old and already I badly wanted to be in a different place, time and person.

Harvey and NDG are permanently connected. Not only did he become a famous NDG boy, but Harvey lived there his entire life and was often seen on a local rink helping kids with their hockey fundamentals. After he died, they named a local arena after him. There are worse things for a community to brag about than a hockey player (Edmonton brags about a shopping mall and Toronto shows off a massive, concrete, phallic-shaped tower), but what did it mean? What was NDG celebrating? Harvey gave a lot to the kids in the community, but what did all the on-ice tips mean without perspective? Did

Harvey ever tell the kids to make sure they got an education or, at the very least, remind them that hockey wouldn't last forever, that they'd have to think of their lives beyond those few years? Of course he didn't, because he didn't really believe that hockey wouldn't last forever. More than the alcoholism or the manic depression, this illusion would be his biggest downfall.

My hockey obsession continued well into my late teens. I played road or ice hockey whenever I could and rarely missed a Habs game on radio or TV. When I was in a groove, all I wanted to do was play. It didn't matter what position, though I refused to play goal without, at the very least, a goalie stick (preferably a Vic like Gilles Gilbert used). Playing without goalies sucked, but not having nets wasn't much better. Without the netting, posts or crossbar we couldn't gloat over the precision of our shots. I was a shy person but for hockey I would go door to door to find people to play. When we played, the world shut down. We existed in this moment and that was that.

Maybe I played better knowing that I really didn't want to be a hockey player. Street hockey wasn't real hockey anyway. If I played ice hockey maybe my poor skating would be exposed. Hell, I couldn't even take a slapshot on the ice. But off the ice, I was great: I always had a knack for scoring, always knew where to be. But if anyone asked me to explain it, I couldn't. It was instinctual. I never thought about technique when I went home, never tinkered with the amount of tape on my stick, never worked on my shots. I just lost myself in the intensity of the moment and that was that. Playing on an ice hockey team would have meant responsibility. It would have meant drills, lots of boring figure eights and skating end to end, through pylons, doing crossovers, backwards, whatever. I didn't want that, I wanted fame *now*. I didn't want to waste time with this dull stuff. Practice makes perfect my ass. Shut up and let me play.

In NDG, the Montreal Royals hockey organization sponsored many of the teams. In return, they got the inside scoop on which players to watch. The Royals personnel then relayed their information to the Montreal Canadiens. If a boy showed a flicker of promise he was added to their negotiation list.

Up to his late teens, it wasn't even clear that Harvey would make it in hockey. He was a stubborn player who liked to carry the puck too much. He did not heed advice well and often looked like he was floating around the ice in circles. Harvey didn't distinguish himself until his last year of high school (an extra year at that) when he helped lead West Hill to the provincial hockey championship. After high school, Harvey signed up for the Navy and was assigned to the Navy hockey team, Donnacona. From 1942 to 1944, Harvey played for both the Navy and the Quebec Junior Hockey League. "I was amazed," said Dickie Moore, who played with the Junior Royals. "He used to come in with his Navy uniform, get out and play for the juniors." In 1944, Harvey helped lead the Montreal Jr. Royals to the Memorial Cup championship.

By now people were becoming aware of Doug Harvey and the Montreal Royals senior team even invited him to suit up for them on a few occasions. "I played for the Canadiens farm team, the Royals," says Red Storey, "and we went on an exhibition tour to New York and Boston one year. Doug was playing junior and we took him with us. We found out how good he was!"

"He stood out like a beacon," adds former Canadiens defenceman and assistant general manager Ken Reardon. "There was no doubt when you went to see him. You'd say, 'Who's that?' and they'd say, 'Doug Harvey.' You stood up and took notice."

From the spring of 1944 till the summer of 1945, Harvey's sporting life was put on hold while he served on Merchant Navy ships. After the war ended, Harvey headed for his first Montreal Canadiens training camp in September 1945. He was assigned to the Montreal Royals of the Quebec Senior League, where he played until 1947.

After a dominating performance – highlighted by some spectacular rushes – that led the Royals to the 1947 Allan Cup, Harvey headed to the Canadiens camp in September and, for a moment, made the team.

While there was no doubt about Harvey's talent, there were always concerns about his attitude. Harvey had a tough time going through the ranks. He was not only undisciplined, but also lazy and stubborn. He wanted to do things his way and, apparently, annoying others didn't faze him. Just shut up, give me the puck, and let me play. As with school, coaches couldn't teach Harvey. He was going to be his own man no matter what. His attitude alienated a few, and despite his success with the Royals and almost everyone's belief that he would be an NHL star, it would take a few years before Harvey lived up to the hype.

In later years, teammates, writers and friends all speculated on when it was that Doug Harvey's life began to spiral downhill. Some talk about the trade from the Canadiens to the Rangers in 1961; others say it was when he was cut by the Rangers in 1963; a few more say that it wasn't any particular time, it was just in his nature to follow his own path. They're all wrong. Doug Harvey's life began to spiral the moment he defined his life through sport.

He wasn't alone. Many boys had the same mentality, thinking sports would last a lifetime. Few of them realized that it was but a fragment of their lives. Doug Harvey was more fortunate than most. Hockey would camouflage him for the next twenty to thirty years as a player, coach and scout. But eventually, he'd have to confront himself.

THE MAUSOLEUM
OF HOPE AND DESIRE

"… those guys who once seemed to walk on water are falling
in front of me … I had always been so sure of everything.
Now it was hard to make sense of a lot of situations."

—Dave "Tiger" Williams

April 2003. It's playoff time. Canadian Tire is selling Ottawa
Senators flags that attach to the car window. A small part of
me wants to participate in the rah-rahness of it all. Hundreds
upon hundreds of cars are adorned with these small black
flags: "Hey, look at me, I'm an Ottawa Senators fan!"

Whatever my feelings about the flag-carrying fools, hockey
does have a communal power. It brings people together.
When Doug Harvey played, the Montreal Canadiens were
the cultural army of French Canada. Each victory was a slap
to the head of the wealthy *anglais.* Is it that different from, for
example, the recent Ottawa–Toronto games? Ottawa may be
the capital in name and politics, but Toronto holds the keys
to the bank. Toronto is loathed by the rest of the country.
Each Ottawa or Vancouver or Calgary win over the Maple
Leafs is also a symbolic victory over the perceived wealthy
arrogance of Toronto.

The fact that we even have an NHL team in Ottawa inspires
confidence and, in many ways, helps Ottawa economically by

carrying the city's name across the world. Players like Marian Hossa, Martin Havlat, Wade Redden and Daniel Alfredsson are role models to a lot of young boys, who now dream of living in Ottawa and wearing Ottawa Senators uniforms. On the surface these are seemingly impotent gestures, but there is some potency present. Victories inspire confidence communally and individually. In Ottawa, the Senators were initially a terrible team. They were losers. This coincided with a decade of enduring a losing football team, the Ottawa Rough Riders. Confidence was low. But since the Senators started winning, you could feel the surge of confidence throughout the city. A winning team makes the day a little bit more bearable.

I became a Montreal Canadiens fan in the mid-seventies. It had nothing to do with history, tradition, torches or any of that romantic claptrap. They were winners. I wanted to be a winner. Before that, I was a Bruins fan. But, despite having a damn good team, the Bruins kept losing. I got tired of it. I especially got tired of watching them lose to Montreal. So that was it, I became a turncoat. From then on, I followed the Canadiens obsessively, from their four straight cups through to the dark days of the present. Over that time, the relationship became more mature. Tradition began to outweigh winning because I'd made emotional, physical, economic and intellectual investments in the team: I watched or listened to every game I could; I made the occasional trip to Montreal to see a game; I followed all the daily happenings and stats; I had a Canadiens jersey.

The relationship soured a few years ago. Ottawa finally got their own NHL team and, as they became increasingly successful, I started to embrace them over Montreal. It wasn't hard. Montreal was a mediocre team hampered by injuries, economics and years of questionable decisions that were, ironically, made because of tradition and history rather than logic. There were times when the team didn't know when to stop embracing the past. They hired coaches and managers because they were ex-players. They signed and traded for players because they were French Canadian. Too often they gave credence to what the fans and media thought. All bad moves. The team fell near the bottom of the league.

In 2002, they snuck into the playoffs and, despite the success of the Ottawa Senators, I found myself reconnecting with the Habs. Sure it was about winning, but it was about something else, too. There was a feeling there that you couldn't find with other teams. I remember a camera panning across the arena after Montreal upset, appropriately enough, Boston. People were crying. It was unbelievable. It was pathetic. It was moving. Sure it had been an emotional season: the team had been sold to an American; team captain Saku Koivu had been diagnosed with cancer; another player, Donald Audette, came close to losing his life earlier in the season during a freak on-ice accident. During the first half of the season, the team pretty much stank. But things began to change: young goaltender Jose Theodore was suddenly unbeatable and, after the dreadful start, the team pulled off an incredible late-season winning streak to sneak into the playoffs for the first time in years. As if that wasn't enough, Saku Koivu vigorously fought off cancer and returned to the team (as did Audette) just in time for the playoffs.

There really was something special about it all. Not only were lifelong Canadien haters rooting for the team, but so were opposing clubs (sort of). When the Canadiens were down 8–2 to Carolina and on the verge of elimination not only did fans stand up to applaud the team but, more incredibly, even the Carolina players began tapping their sticks in appreciation for what the team had overcome during the season. Truth be told, the Canadiens had not really endured anything that other teams hadn't been through. But this was the Montreal Canadiens, the Habs, the *Trois Couleurs*, the Flying Frenchmen – the gods of hockey lore. The reaction that night and all season long would not happen in any other rink, for any other team.

How did the Montreal Canadiens come to symbolize such power and mystique? Timing. There is no more important element to life than timing. You can plan all you want, but if the timing doesn't come together, you got nothin'.

In 1909, the National Hockey Association was comprised of English Canadian teams (Renfrew, Ottawa, Cobalt, Haileybury and Montreal) and rich English Canadian owners. In order to strengthen the league and ensure its survival the owners craved a French Canadian team. There was already a team in Montreal named the Wanderers, but they attracted predominantly English fans. A French team would provide a rivalry for the Wanderers and ideally attract the interest and cash of the French Canadian population. Under the guidance of, oddly enough, an English millionaire named Ambrose O'Brien, the Club de Hockey Canadien was born. O'Brien's stint was short. The owner (George Kendall) of a French-speaking sports club, Club Athlétique Canadien, already had dibs on the Club Canadien name. The shrewd NHA owners saw no point in going to court over the matter because, more to the point, they figured that the members of Kendall's club would very likely become devoted hockey fans. Kendall was given ownership of the Club de Hockey Canadien.

Things did not go as expected. After three seasons, the Canadiens dropped their French-player-only rule. And despite winning the Stanley Cup in 1916, they never captured the imagination of Montreal's French population. In fact, attendance got so bad during the Depression that there was even talk of moving the franchise to Cleveland. The team had spurts of success (1929–31) and a couple of superstars in Howie Morenz (Morenz's popularity led to American expansion in Detroit, Boston and New York) and Aurel Joliat, but it wasn't until the mid-1940s and the arrival of Maurice Richard that the team began to take on a mythological mystique.

Richard's fiery eyes, almost psychotic drive, routinely spectacular goals and working-class roots captured the hearts of the French Canadians. Some writers suggest that Richard's true arrival occurred in March 1944, when he scored all five goals in a playoff game against Toronto. The following season, Richard was all over the front pages while he chased and eclipsed Joe Malone's long-time goal-scoring record (the equivalent of Babe Ruth's sixty home runs).

Even then, it was timing. Richard's fierce, impassioned play captured fans during a turbulent time. Like other Canadians, Quebecers had suffered through a severe economic depression that only ended when world war broke out. The war was not popular in Quebec. Many Quebecois felt that this was Europe's war and that Canada had no business fighting in it. When Prime Minister Mackenzie King's conscription law passed, tensions between English and French Canada heightened. For the French, this was yet another example of the arrogant English dictating what they should do. To make matters worse, Quebec was under the control of its own dictator, Maurice Duplessis. During his eighteen years as premier (starting in 1936), his paranoid, intolerant policies helped turn Quebec into an impoverished, almost backwater province. After decades of church, state and Anglo oppression, Quebec was on the edge of eruption.

Richard's determined and violent play came to symbolize the frustration of French Canadians. And through Richard, Quebec unleashed its communal rage against the world. The volcano finally erupted in 1955 when the fans rioted the streets of Montreal after the English-speaking NHL President, Clarence Campbell, suspended Richard for the entire playoffs for slugging an on-ice official. There are some who believe that the "Richard Riot" opened the door for Quebec's Quiet Revolution of the 1960s and 1970s, which, in essence, actively sought to preserve, protect and strengthen the voice of Quebec in Canada.

There is little doubt that Maurice Richard fed the myth, but it wasn't his alone. His career also happened to coincide with the emergence of what would be one of the most successful sports franchises in history. Over the course of twenty-five years (1955–80), the Canadiens won fifteen Stanley Cup championships, including a still-unbeaten five in a row from 1955 to 1960.

The Canadiens now transcend hockey. Like the New York Yankees, fans and non-fans alike universally recognize the Canadiens. Today, however, the myth is less about ghosts, winning and heroes than it is about marketing. The mythology of the Canadiens has been very carefully maintained and recreated by public relations departments. The Canadiens are now a corporation, a product no different from Disney, Time-Warner or Microsoft. History and tradition have been repackaged as commodities to be bought, sold, traded and collected.

And we're not talking marketing just to the fans and public, the Canadiens marketed the myth to the players as well. Both the old Montreal Forum and its replacement arena, the Bell Centre, are adorned with reminders of the past. The Canadiens dressing room became famous because of the photos of old players placed along the tops of the walls. Beneath the photos were the famous words (from the poem, "In Flanders Fields"): "To you from failing hands we throw / The torch; be yours to hold it high."

More than any other franchise, except maybe Disney, the team has never let the past slip away into the amnesia of history. On any given night you'll see a Habs oldtimer at the game or a special ceremony being held to honour a personality or team from the past. Various championship and player banners hang from the arena rafters.

Despite icing some weak teams during the 1980s and 1990s, the power and impact of the club, as evidenced during the 2002 playoffs, remains strong. With expansion and parity, however, it's unlikely that Montreal will ever see a roster of the calibre they've come to expect. Perhaps the fans know this. Why else would they show such an incredible outpouring (off-ice distractions aside) of emotion over something so minor as a second round playoff appearance (a feat demanded of the team in past decades)? Perhaps it was something else too – a momentary injection of light or hope in a new century and a new world. It seems silly, really, that a hockey game could have so much meaning, but as the sweeping sameness of global culture continues to raze uniqueness and difference, a victory, any victory, however small or impotent, is sometimes just about the best Quebec and Canada can hope for.

Doug Harvey, I'm told, was a great hockey player. What does it mean to be a great hockey player, let alone a great NHL hockey player? How do we define the greatest players in the world anyway? What about those many players who were never given a chance for a variety of political, personal, racial and economic reasons? What about all those years of the non-European NHL? Just look at how dominant Russians and Europeans are in the league today. Many countries like Sweden, Finland and Russia have long hockey histories, but because the doors were closed to them, their players of the past are barely acknowledged. Too often fans and media exude an unconscious ignorance, a willingness to perpetuate the myth of the NHL as hockey. In truth, money and media define the great.

Athletes are the most complete artists. Unlike writers or painters or studio musicians, all their performances are unedited. We see everything in their work: the good, bad, ugly, the brilliant and irrelevant.

History is created by people who weren't there.

My wife can't get into hockey. She says it's because she isn't intimate with the teams. She's not aware of their positions in the standings, their histories, let alone any of the players. She just sees anonymous figures moving back and forth across the television screen in search of something she can't even see.

Doug Harvey's early years were filled with Canadiens connections: he fled the womb just weeks after the Montreal Forum hosted its first hockey game; goalie Bill Durnan's house was one of the stops on Harvey's paper route (Harvey would sometimes try and sneak a peek at Durnan in his living room); and Harvey attended the famous Howie Morenz funeral held in the Forum in 1937.

After leading the Montreal Royals to the Allan Cup in 1947, Harvey went to the Canadiens training camp that fall and made the team as a fifth defenceman. His stay, however, was short. He'd had it so good with the Montreal Royals, he just figured it would be more of the same with the Canadiens, so he showed up overweight and with a lazy attitude. "I remember him," says Ken Reardon of Harvey's debut. "He wasn't an instant success. He had a funny style. If everyone else was playing like hell, he'd go slow on purpose to show them this game isn't that tough."

Because Harvey had played fifty to sixty minutes a game with the Royals, he had learned how to conserve his energy. He paced himself so that he could play an entire game. If a game was out of reach, he didn't bother playing hard. If it was close, he was a superstar. This was fine in the senior league, but not in the NHL. Canadiens coaches, teammates and fans saw it as laziness. You were expected to go all out, all the time.

"When I first came up to Canadiens, I was just a fifth defenceman," Harvey said in an October 1960 article in

Hockey Pictorial magazine. "But I had a good reputation from my days with the Royals, so I took it easy. I began taking on weight and I looked lousy. Next thing you know, I'm playing for Buffalo." After thirty-five games, he was sent down to Montreal's minor league team, the Buffalo Bisons.

Having his ego slapped woke Harvey up. "I had enough in one season at Buffalo. We used to travel thirty-five miles to St. Catharines to practice. When we got there half the players hadn't had breakfast so they'd go and eat while the other half practiced. Then we'd switch. No sir, I had enough of the minors."

By February 1948, Harvey was up with the Canadiens for good. Even then, Harvey spent the next few seasons routinely frustrating fans, coaches and teammates with his lack of consistency and his easygoing style on the ice. "Most players will say they play 110 percent," says Ken Reardon, "but Harvey was always 100 percent and he gave me the impression that he couldn't go any higher. He'd be doing it in such a lackadaisical fashion. I often thought that if this guy would get interested in this game he'd be a tremendous hockey player. He still was a tremendous hockey player but there was room for a lot more from him. I don't know why he couldn't do it."

One of Harvey's biggest, unacknowledged, problems in those early years was the very same Ken Reardon. Reardon was a rough, loud, cocky player and he didn't like Harvey from the start. Reardon was a leader among a core of firmly established and intimidating veterans that included Toe Blake, Rocket Richard and Butch Bouchard. They were a close-knit bunch and Harvey was essentially an outsider. This was probably not the ideal situation for a shy, aw-shucks kinda guy like Harvey. As much as he was a do-it-yourself man, he also wanted acceptance from his teammates, wanted to be part of the pack. His on-ice play reflected his shyness. He appeared lazy and apathetic to many fans and they showered him with boos. "It's just my manner of play I guess," Harvey told Len Bramson in a 1950 *Hockey News* story. "I admit I let down a bit now and then but don't think that I'm not out there giving my best. The fans like to see a defenceman rushing up and down the ice all night but you can't do that against every club."

While Harvey maintained until his dying day that his game never changed one bit during his career, some journalists and teammates felt otherwise. Most people suggest that Reardon's retirement prior to the 1950–51 season elevated Harvey's game. "He always had that great ability," says former Canadien defenceman Tom Johnson, "but for some reason when he first joined the Canadiens they had a pretty cliquey group there and he wasn't part of it. There might have been some tension between Harvey and Reardon near the end of Reardon's days because Doug was the rising star." Harvey probably wouldn't admit to being intimidated by Reardon, and statistically speaking he was right. The year after Reardon retired, Harvey's offensive totals only jumped from 24 to 29 points. Still, whatever the motivation, Harvey's play improved. He made smarter decisions with the puck and played with more confidence. "I gained a measure of success last season," admitted Harvey, "from the fact that for the first time I felt I was the number one defenceman on the club. It gave me a sense of responsibility." By October 1950, *The Hockey News* was hailing Harvey as "the best defenceman on the team."

Television defines our perception of hockey today. But this is a relatively recent phenomenon. Prior to the arrival of Canadian sports networks like TSN, Sportsnet and the Score (which didn't really reach mass audiences until the mid-nineties), most of us knew hockey primarily through radio. With the exception of the playoffs, *Hockey Night in Canada* was a one-night-a-week gig. And as powerless kids, even then there was no guarantee that we'd be allowed to watch one period let alone all three. And highlights? Forget it. Unless you happened to sit through one of those dull CJOH and CBOT newscasts in Ottawa, you would never catch a glimpse of the night's action.

No, the only way to stay in touch with hockey was through radio. In Ottawa, we received every Montreal Canadiens game broadcast. For the decade or so that I fanatically listened, Dick Irvin was the eyes, ears, and voice of my hockey experience. I let nothing get in the way of these broadcasts. Homework was put aside and social calls were cut short. And if a game clashed with one of my babysitting jobs, I got that kid to sleep as soon as the parents were out the door so I wouldn't miss one minute.

Before every broadcast, I got out my pencil and 8" x 11"

school notebook. I drew a line down the middle and at the top wrote down the name of the two teams playing that night. In these two columns I wrote down every goal and assist from the game. At the bottom of the page I made a separate column for penalty minutes (usually reserved for Chris Nilan) and goals against (either Rick Walmsley, Richard Sevigny or Denis Herron were between the pipes). And at the end of journal I kept track of the overall Canadiens team-scoring race (Acton, Napier and Lafleur were battling for top spot). The experience was so precious that I even started recording entire games on some shitty tape recorder so I could replay seemingly spectacular goals any time. The goal didn't really matter. It was the roar of the Forum crowd and that distinctive organ tune, my anthem of the 1980s.

It's little wonder that hockey cards and sticker books were so important to us as kids because, aside from a few NHL yearbooks or assorted kid-oriented biographies, they were really our sole visual access to the players. Through street hockey and hockey cards we made our own highlight reels. Through them we recreated what we imagined our heroes were doing on the radio.

Given *Hockey Night in Canada*'s mythological status in Canada, television is a poor way to watch a hockey game. The game is too fast for television cameras. As the cameras struggle to keep up they invariably reduce, obscure and silence many parts of the play. On television, the puck is the protagonist. Goals, saves, bodychecks and fights are given emphasis. The assorted defensive and offensive plays that lead to those highlight-reel moments are usually unseen and, subsequently, unheralded. Often, the most important plays in hockey are happening away from the puck. Television's emphasis on puck movement often confused inexperienced viewers. They couldn't see it, let alone follow. FOX-TV's glowing puck experiment in the late 1990s is a case in point. The network gave the puck a bluish hue to make it easier for viewers to see (to their credit, though, FOX and ABC also introduced new camera angles – specifically the camera that tracked side-to-side behind the net – that added fresh perspectives of the game).

At the same time, television has also slowed down the game. Despite the League's recent initiatives for quicker faceoffs, play is still halted for one or two minutes while the networks run commercials. While these breaks can give a team a much-needed rest, they take away any momentum.

The retarded pace along with market pressures has also changed the dynamics of the hockey broadcasts. Because they are covering more and more games, many of which are far from entertaining, the network must ensure that the illusion of drama is a constant fixture during a broadcast so that they don't lose viewers, and with them, advertising dollars. So while the commentators ramble on and on citing meaningless statistics or making the most staggeringly obvious observations, the director tries to generate tension through close-ups of emotional coaches, players and fans. Television has turned hockey into a soap opera where our emotions and reactions are dictated to us.

This manufactured hype is also prominent in hockey literature, a field that has rapidly expanded over the last ten to fifteen years. With few exceptions (such as Richard Gruneau and David Whitson's *Hockey Night in Canada: Sports, Identities and Cultural Politics*, Douglas Hunter's *Open Ice: The Tim Horton Story*, Roch Carrier's *Our Life with the Rocket*, Georges-Hebert Germain's *Overtime: The Legend of Guy Lafleur*, Chrys Goyens and Allan Turowetz's *Lions in Winter*, Tiger Williams's *Tiger: A Hockey Story*, Alison Griffiths and David Cruise's *Net Worth: Exploding the Myths of Pro Hockey* and Mark Anthony Jarman's brilliant hockey novel, *Salvage King, Ya!*) hockey writing reflects this tendency to see the sport as an island disconnected from the pressures, responsibilities and effects of the real world.

Hockey literature is saturated with well-meaning but superficial anecdotal "histories" that reduce the player's life to a series of lengthy and very dull game-by-game summaries. Most of these hagiographies speak the same stories about needing to grow up more, about using frozen horse shit for a puck, about sacrifices their parents made, about career-threatening injuries or conflicts with a coach, about the pursuit of the cup or trophy. Then comes the tortured, romanticized moment when a player knows it's time to hang up the blades, followed by the grand old summary about how grand their lives were and how they have no regrets WHATSOEVER. The stories are all so familiar that it seems like these guys had lived the same life. It was as if a player had lived his entire existence on a televised skating rink.

Even with the new responsibility and encouragement, Harvey remained inconsistent. By January 1951, it looked certain that Harvey would either be sent to the minor leagues or traded. The Canadiens were having an awful season (they ended up finishing below .500) and Harvey became the target. He was taking too many penalties and the fans were booing him mercilessly for his seemingly nonchalant play. As one reporter noted, "'Sleepy Time Gal' could have been played while he waltzed through each session." The February trade deadline came and went and Harvey remained a Hab. Just when it seemed certain (at least in the media's eyes) that he would be sent to the minors, Harvey put together a solid series of games in March and led the team into the playoffs.

Debate over Harvey's play continued throughout the early fifties. Len Bramson of *The Hockey News* felt that Harvey was ahead of everyone else: "He is one of the few players in hockey today who has the complete coordination of mind and body in a game. In other words, he can think and play the game at the same time." Harvey's former Montreal Royals coach Frank Carlin agreed: "Harvey is so confident in himself that he looks as though he isn't hustling. If Doug thinks he can get the puck before the other fellow, he will go just as fast as he feels he has to. The system is fine so long as everything is going well, but as soon as he miscues once, the howl goes up that Harvey isn't trying."

Harvey's coach, Dick Irvin, a man who knew how to motivate, often used the media to send a message to a player.

In 1952, he told *The Hockey News*: "For years I've been hearing that story about Harvey being the best player in the league if he wants to be. Well I'm sick and tired of hearing it. He can't play hockey and I'm going to see that he goes to Mr. Selke and resigns from this club. That guy just can't play hockey."

Irvin was so frustrated with Harvey's style ("he dilly-dallies around his own net with the puck too much") that he imposed a $100 fine (a pretty hefty sum at the time) on Harvey if he ever carried the puck in front of the net and was checked. Typically, Harvey toyed with Irvin. "Nobody ever did [take the puck from me]. I admit that I used take chances. Sometimes I'd cross over in front and look up at the coach. Then I'd go off the ice and sit on the bench and yell, 'Cancel that fine coach, I can't stand the pressure.' The boys used to rip me plenty but it never affected me."

Despite Harvey's apathetic appearance, both Selke and Dick Irvin felt it was a put on. "He drove my father up the wall," says Dick Irvin Jr. "Finally during the first week of February in 1953, Selke and my father met at our house to discuss Harvey's play after a recent game. They felt that Harvey's careless play had resulted in the tying and winning goals. Harvey sat on the bench for the entirety of the next game against the Leafs. Fans started hollering for Harvey when they realized what was happening – even calling my father 'a stubborn old bastard.' The next morning, and what gives us some insight into this supposed cool and apathetic guy, Harvey was on the ice alone practising. When the McGill hockey team came on for their practice [including the young Dick Irvin] Harvey asked to practise with them. Dad always felt that he was a lot more uptight, nervous and caring than he would let on."

Harvey got his revenge in 1952. After being voted as a first team all-star in 1951–52 (the first of eleven consecutive all-star appearances), *The Hockey News* invited Harvey to defend himself in a column. He wrote about how happy he was to be an all-star because it would finally shut up the Montreal critics: "I played the same game last season as the season before, yet one I was a bum and the other I was an all-star. I take offence to some newspapermen who watch you play eight good games and hardly say a word and then take you over the coals when you come up with a bad one."

Still, Harvey freely admitted that he took it easy at times: "I admit that I pace myself a little during a game and that I watch the clock a little more than is maybe good for me, but when I'm in a game and we're a goal up, I'm not out to make any foolish mistakes. Oh, I know I look like I'm playing it dangerously when I play around my own net, but that's the way I play the game. I know what I'm doing back there, believe me…"

"He would dare you to take the puck away from him," adds former Detroit Red Wing Ted Lindsay. "It was like he had a yo-yo and he'd push it out at you and then bring it back."

Harvey hated dumping the puck if he didn't have to because doing so meant that you gave up possession. "I can shoot that puck out of there any time but when that one goal means the difference I'm not throwing any pucks away."

Despite the obvious risks, Harvey's logic makes perfect sense. He was doing what was best for the team.

The success of Harvey's game seemed connected to that of the team. If they were losing, his play would follow suit. He'd look bored and uninterested. When the team was doing well, he was a powerhouse. What made Harvey so unique was that he fused the bipolar (yes, a pun) nature of previous defencemen, those who were either the stay-at-home, conservative types more focused on defending their zone or those who were the more aggressive offensive types who rushed the puck from one end to another and made perfect passes up the rink. Harvey did both equally well. He was a steady checker, but he could also rush up the ice in an instant.

One of his trademarks was the fast, accurate breakout pass to streaking forwards. The forwards had to be moving, though: "I won't give you the puck if you're not skating," Harvey once said. "If you're standing still, if you park yourself near the boards and wait for a pass from me, it won't come. You'll die of old age standing at the boards. If you want the puck, you'll get it on the fly."

As Harvey earned more responsibility, he felt more comfortable with his teammates. "He was basically a quiet man," says ex-teammate and friend Rip Riopelle. "You'd never see him chastise anyone or tell them what they should be doing. He showed it on the ice primarily. He wasn't a rah-rah type of guy."

"When I joined the Canadiens in 1953," says Jean Beliveau, "if we wanted to find out something about the organization or if we had a problem, we always went to Doug. He always took the time to listen and to try to solve it himself or he would contact the proper person in management. He was so good to everyone who needed advice. He was a one-man welcome wagon."

Perhaps Harvey's biggest contribution, aside from his play, was his sense of humour. "He was a non-stop joker," remembers Beliveau in his memoir *My Life in Hockey*, "a happy-go-lucky guy who could always be counted on to lighten the tension during a vital game. When a game didn't count for much in the standings, he'd keep us all in stitches."

"He kept the guys loose," says Dick Irvin Jr. "In Detroit once, the game was heading into a third overtime and he said, 'Come on guys, the bars are gonna close.'"

Irvin Jr. also remembers a notorious gag that Harvey pulled on his father. "Harvey apparently led some players into letting my father's pigeons [Irvin was a pigeon farmer] out of their cages while on a train car. When [my father] arrived the next morning, the players had the birds back in the cage but there were feathers all over the place."

Harvey's antics weren't always for laughs. "Prior to a 1961 playoff game against Chicago," says *Montreal Gazette* columnist, Red Fisher, a close friend of Harvey's, "[Bernie 'Boom Boom'] Geoffrion had been injured. He was with the team but wearing a cast that ran from his ankle to thigh. We were together in a group and Doug was giving Bernie shots about hobbling around on this cast while everyone was playing. Then Doug decided that it would be good if he cut the cast off, which he proceeded to do." Geoffrion dressed for the game but soon found that he was in incredible pain and had to leave the game.

"He was a silent joker with a dry sense of humour," adds Dickie Moore. "One time he drove a Vespa scooter right into the dressing room during training camp."

My favourite story comes from a 1950s exhibition game against the Sudbury Wolves, an Ontario Senior League team. The Canadiens were well ahead of the Wolves, but Sudbury suddenly scored. All of a sudden this wolf mannequin comes flying out from one end of the rink and hovers above the ice surface while the sound of a wolf howl blares through the sound system – apparently this was a common ritual following a Wolves goal. Later in the game, Harvey scored on his own net. After Toe Blake finished blasting Harvey for his foolishness, Harvey turned around, smiled, and said, "Sorry, Toe, but it was worth it just to see that wolf again."

How the hell can I write about Doug Harvey, the hockey player let alone the person, when I didn't even see him play, didn't even meet him? I watched dozens of old Habs games on tape. Honestly, I probably wouldn't have noticed Harvey if I wasn't looking for him. Of course, that's part of his game. He was a defenceman. He did the small things well; he was a master at conserving energy and positioning. On occasion, I'd see one of his smooth rushes up the ice or one of those famous passes to a moving forward, but it's still not the same. You've got to be there, breathing the time, the people and the environment. I had to rely on the memories of teammates, journalists and other writers – some of whom weren't even there either. I watched these old games but felt nothing. First of all, everything is black and white. It's not real. And all the players look so damn old. I swear that Gump Worsley and Johnny Bower were *always* forty-seven years old.

It wasn't just how the games looked, it was more my lack of feeling. I'd be watching playoff games and even though I was familiar with most of the players but had no idea of the games' outcomes, I felt no excitement or tension. Hockey is an emotionally charged sport, but watching these old games gave me none of that. I felt like a scientist coldly analyzing a subject. Nothing more. Maybe that's a good thing. Hockey, like any other sport, has become so emotionally affixed to our lives that we often lack the ability to step back and see it for what it really is, and has been since it became organized: a cold, unemotional business. Many people assume that the NFL, NBA, MBL and NHL are the Mount Olympus of their sports, but they're just the most successful. They're monopolies. Hockey's existence is not in the hands of the National Hockey League.

By 1955, Harvey appeared to find his consistency at about the time the Canadiens gelled as a team. The same year Harvey won the first of seven (over the next eight seasons) Norris Trophies for Best Defenceman, the team won the first of its record five consecutive Stanley Cup championships.

The fans and media soon forgot about "Sleepy Time Gal."
The Hockey News now hailed Harvey with the rhetorical, "Is
Harvey Greatest?" article.

For his part, Harvey felt he never changed his game. "If I
was loafing the year I broke in, I'm loafing now." Red Fisher,
who had known Harvey since the late 1940s, agrees: "I think
people just got Doug's style. He was the same player with the
Montreal Royals. He was just confident. He knew he could
play this game and knew he could play it better than anyone
else at that position at that time."

Myths, myths, myths. We're engulfed by them today. The
word comes from the Greek *mythos*, meaning story or speech.
Most of us associate myths with the Greeks, whose tales of
mighty supernatural gods conveyed messages about the state
of humanity at the time. In short, myth is fiction, akin to
legend, fantasy and hearsay. In his 1957 book *Mythologies*,
French philosopher Roland Barthes examined a variety of
cultural activities (ranging from wrestling and toys to soap
powder and striptease) to argue that myths are not simply an
innocent form of speech about supernatural gods, but rather
an ideological tool used to promote the beliefs and values of
the speaker.

In our modern myths, used in every form of mass media
and popular culture today, beliefs and values are presented
as something inherent and universal; alternative forms of
thought are ridiculed or simply ignored. Advertising is

perhaps the most obvious example of a modern myth. It's a world where conflict, when it is present, is easily contained and resolved by a process of equivocation.

I think it was Joseph Goebbels who said that if you repeated something enough people would start to believe it as truth.

Hockey, like almost every arena of our lives, is full of myths. The most recurrent hockey myth suggests that when the National Hockey League had only six teams (deemed the "Original Six" for years now), it was a more genuine, magical world where everyone was of the humble, gosh-golly-gee, Mayberry variety. So often we hear the phrases "the golden years" in connection with that time (1942–67). "The Original Six NHL," our grandpops tell us, "was about the game, it wasn't about money. Furthermore," Gramps prattles on, "those boys knew how to play back then. They weren't greedy or violent. It's just wrestling on ice today."

Gramps, of course, like most hockey "historians" who drone out the same stories, is delusional. Then as now, the NHL was a racket. The NHL has always been a profit-seeking business. In the Original Six days, it was just a simpler, more basic, but no less ambitious racket.

From an economic standpoint, it's been well-documented how the Original Six owners bullied the players into submission. The owners played off hockey's mythological powers and kept salaries low. They'd remind players that it wasn't about the money, that it was about this beautiful game: "You should be damn glad to get paid to play hockey. Lots of kids would love to be in your shoes." Owners like Detroit's Bruce Norris would tell players that he wasn't in it for the money, but for the love of the game (and while there might be a dash of truth to that, it's only because the Norris family also had stakes in the Black Hawks and the Rangers, and controlled most of US boxing).

The players, except guys like Harvey and Ted Lindsay, believed it. When they didn't, they were threatened. There was no players' association in those days and a player could be cut or demoted in an instant. The players had absolutely no power. To make matters worse, fraternizing with opponents or discussing salaries was frowned upon. Most of them were poorly educated, small-town boys. They grew up in an era when you respected your elders. Owners were kings and you didn't fuck with them.

And worse still, a lot of these players couldn't live all year on their hockey salaries and had to find summer jobs to supplement their incomes. Leafs owner Conn Smythe masked himself as a good guy by offering some players summer jobs with his construction company. Gee, what a swell fella. The gesture ensured player loyalty, while providing more cheap labour for Smythe.

It was the players who made the NHL successful and yet they were treated like puppets. And when their careers ended, many of them didn't have a dime to show for it. Yes, there was a pension fund but it was never enough to live on. In the 1990s a series of books appeared (Bruce Dowbiggin's *The Defence Never Rests*, Ross Conway's *Game Misconduct*, and Alison Griffiths and David Cruise's *Net Worth*) which dug through the layers of myth to discover that the owners (and players' association boss, Alan Eagleson) had in fact been stealing from the players' pension fund for years. Hall of Fame players had been collecting peanuts. Howe was getting $13,000 a year, Richard $7000 and Orr $8400 (all Canadian dollars).

And those were the superstars. As Brian McFalone's book *Over the Glass and into the Crowd!: Life After Hockey* shows, many players ended up in low-paying jobs or doing assorted appearances and signings at card shows or shopping malls because they needed money and/or had no formal education or career training. The NHL did little to help players adapt to life after hockey.

Harvey was one of those guys who knew he was being screwed. Since the early fifties, he'd irritate general manager Selke by continually holding off signing his contract until the last possible minute. Harvey knew he wasn't going to get more money, and he didn't necessarily want more money; he simply resented the idea that these people effectively owned him. Ken Reardon, who by this time was the Canadiens' assistant manager, had a different view: "He was holding out on contracts because he could. It wasn't about more money. He was trying to figure out a better way to do it. He always had a better way to do it. We were gonna eat at 7 pm, he'd want to eat at 6 pm."

In 1955, Harvey (who was the Canadiens' player representative), along with Ted Lindsay, was appointed to the NHL's five-member Pension Society board. The other three representatives were NHL President Clarence Campbell, General John Kilpatrick (a mouthpiece for the notorious Norris family) and Ian S. Johnston, a lawyer for Maple Leaf

Gardens. Both players took the job seriously, but soon found that their many questions were not being answered. Fuelling their frustration was Clarence Campbell's smug legalese. "He used to come and visit us once a year," Lindsay said in the book, *Net Worth*. "When he was through speaking… everybody would say, 'What did he say?'"

After one meeting, Harvey and Lindsay went for beers and discussed their salaries (no one did this at the time). Pretty soon the two men were calculating various figures and soon realized that the owners had been feeding them a line. Hockey was highly profitable and the players were being cheated out of a fair share.

In the summer of 1956, Lindsay happened to meet Cleveland Indians pitcher Bob Feller. Feller had formed the baseball players' association. After Lindsay explained what he and Harvey had uncovered, Feller set up a meeting with New York lawyers Milton Mound and Norman Lewis, who had represented the baseball players. Lindsay met with the New York lawyers and soon agreed that an NHL player's association was necessary. "Once I decided to do it," recalls Lindsay, "I had to make sure that I had the Toronto Maple Leafs and Montreal Canadiens or I wasn't going to get off first base. I can't remember the circumstances which we [Harvey] first started to talk, but I knew I had to get to him. The Rocket was the leader in terms of talent, but Harvey was the leader of that team. Harvey was a very intelligent guy. He didn't talk to hear himself talk. He would say something that meant something."

Lindsay approached Harvey in October 1956 during a pre-game skate of the all-star game. Harvey agreed to help Lindsay and soon they also had the support of captains from the Rangers (Bill Gadsby), Black Hawks (Gus Mortson), Bruins (Fern Flaman) and Maple Leafs (Jimmy Thomson). This was quite an achievement. Unlike players today, the Original-Six players rarely socialized. A widely told story involving Doug Harvey provides a perfect example of what the attitude towards opposing players was: "We're in Detroit," says Red Fisher. "We're not due to travel until Monday night, so we had all day Sunday and Monday. [Coach Toe] Blake decides they should tour the Ford factory. The bus stops in front of the Red Wings' arena, the Olympia. Harvey asks why we're stopping here. Blake says that the Red Wings are coming with us. Harvey says, 'Fuck that, those guys tried to take my head off last night. You think I'm gonna go on a goddamn tour with them today. Fuck you Blake.' He gets up, walks to the front of the bus and gets off. Toe never said a word. Now Toe was feared by the players, some of them thought he could beat them up. But Harvey got off the bus and he didn't make it to the midnight train until about a minute before midnight. And he was staggering drunk. First, he didn't mind drinking, but second, he was pissed off that Toe would even think of inviting the Red Wings."

On February 11, 1957, Lindsay, Harvey and the other players held a press conference in New York announcing the formation of the National Hockey League Players' Association. Harvey was named as the first vice-president.

The owners were stunned, but they reacted hard and fast. Aside from discrediting Lindsay in the press by showing a contract that showed Lindsay making $25,000 per year (which wasn't the truth – Lindsay only made $12,000) the owners bullied the players. Conn Smythe banished Jimmy Thomson from the Leafs and on July 24, 1957, Jack Adams (Detroit's general manager) stunned Red Wings fans when he traded Lindsay to Chicago. While Lindsay and the other team captains were punished for their actions, the Canadiens were not so hasty. "Frank Selke was a smart man," adds Lindsay. "He knew that Doug had about four to five more years. He might not have wanted the player's association, but he wanted Harvey's talent. That's where Adams was stupid. They get rid of me and Glenn Hall and spend the next sixteen years looking for a goaltender. Selke wasn't so anti-association that he wouldn't keep Harvey." The Canadiens were also in the midst of winning five Cups and only a few years earlier during the Richard Riot, Selke had seen what Montreal fans could do when they were unhappy. Harvey remained a Canadien, for the time being.

By September 1957, according to Griffiths and Cruise, there was a thirty-two percent changeover in players. By February 1958, just under a year since Lindsay's press conference, the association was dead and buried. It would finally be reborn in 1967 under the charge of a lawyer named Alan Eagleson. Two decades after that, it would be discovered that Eagleson stole millions of dollars from the players, the people he was supposed to be representing.

In truth, these "sordid" tales of exploitation need to be taken with a grain of salt, too. Whatever the level of greed and arrogance motivating the desires of owners and managers, we must also be careful not to denounce these men as disciples of Satan. If we take away their humanity (as the TV movie *Net Worth* chose to do with the Original Six owners and Jack Adams), they become little more than hockey card caricatures. To call the players innocent, pure and good is just as foolhardy as deeming the owners and management cold-hearted villains. Life is not so neat.

Those who elevate hockey's past are often confusing their youth with hockey. It wasn't hockey that was pure and innocent, it was the child of those times – boys who had very clear, uncomplicated views of hockey and its "heroes." Players weren't human to a boy. Through young eyes, players were like comic book heroes without layers or complexities. It was no different from what we saw of Superman, the Green Lantern, Flash or any other comic book heroes. We just saw the extremes of their lives, the highlight reel. No one ever asked or cared if Superman took a shit or how much money he made as Clark Kent. All we cared about was Superman beating the tar out of Lex Luthor or some other villain.

Hockey was no different. We didn't see these guys as humans, let alone workers. They were just the luckiest fellas in the world because all they did was hang out on the ice all day. What a fantastic life! We didn't know that these guys were like our parents and neighbours, that they played around on their wives, or beat their kids, or drank in alleyways, or spent time in fear of losing their jobs.

Every player I spoke with (even Ken Reardon) praised
Harvey's play. "There was no one like him the NHL," says
former Harvey teammate Billy Reay. "Certainly Bobby Orr
was the greatest offensive defenceman in the NHL, but Doug
was better defensively. He was tough but not dirty. He had
a very heavy shot and was a great point man. He was very
heady and smart. He was a terrific passer – when he passed
the puck, it was on your stick, not in your skates. No player
could go down on his knees and then up on his skates faster
than Doug, so he could block shots and get the puck to you
brilliantly. When I played with Doug, we used to say to him
'What kind of a game are we going to play tonight – fast or
slowed down?' He could control the tempo."

"Harvey can do everything [Eddie] Shore [considered the
premier defenceman before Harvey came along] could do and
some things Shore couldn't do, and make it look easy" former
Canadiens player and coach Toe Blake once said.

"He was the greatest defenceman that ever played, and
that includes Orr," says Ted Lindsay. "Harvey controlled the
Rocket, Beliveau, Geoffrion, Dickie Moore, Olmstead. When
they were on the power play, he was the maestro."

Many rated Harvey and Orr as the greatest defencemen
to ever play in the NHL. But what does that mean? How do
you measure the success of a player who played in another
time under different conditions? Was he even the best of his
time? What about Red Kelly of the Red Wings and Leafs,
Pierre Pilote of the Black Hawks, or Tim Horton of the

Maple Leafs? Did Harvey draw more notice because he was accompanied by an extraordinary lineup of players or did being surrounded by this kind of talent merely allow Harvey's 'pacing' to go unnoticed? Kelly and Pilote played for pretty decent teams but neither of them matched the power of the Canadiens. Even Harvey felt he was lucky: "Heck it's easy to play on this club. All I have to do here is pass the puck to fellows like Maurice Richard, Bernie Geoffrion and Jean Beliveau and they put it in the net."

Perhaps Red Fisher sums up Harvey's career best: "Harvey always lived on the edge, whether it was waiting until the last possible split-second to make a winning pass, or holding out on signing a contract until the last day of training camp. He was stubborn, aggravating, unselfish, hard-drinking, fun-loving and the best defenceman, by far, in Canadiens history."

"Survivor," "hero" and "warrior" are overused and misused words. Hockey scribes – given to hyperbole – use these words to describe hockey players as though the players were fighting for their lives. Some even call hockey a war, a sign that our society has become a little too cozy in a land where war is a distant memory. Maurice Richard, Wayne Gretzky, Gordie Howe, Doug Harvey and many other fine hockey players were not, and are not, heroes.

The problem with the heroism label is that it weeds out all the complexities of a person to showcase all that is perceived to be worthy and good. And, of course, this can be a good thing. It inspires us, gives us motivation to improve ourselves. Assuming that there is something wrong with us … and this is where we run into trouble. Why do we have to improve ourselves? What is so fundamentally wrong with us? Isn't the supposed uniqueness of hockey stars such as Doug Harvey and Rocket Richard what makes them "heroes" to begin with? They weren't like everyone else and that's what made them appealing. But heroism, to a degree, seems to remove the uniqueness with its sweeping blow of sameness.

As Heraclitus bitched, "The poet was a fool who wanted no conflict between us, gods and people." Of course heroism was about conflict, about overcoming obstacles. But the very word heroism has its roots in fiction. Hesiod and Homer were the first poets to write about powerful gods and men at war. Heraclitus didn't like their fantasies. It was a disservice to men to turn them into fantasy, or to turn a complex, often illogical and absurd world into something linear, coherent and meaningful. For Heraclitus, life was a mixture of conflict and harmony, a never-ending cycle that sometimes had a purpose and sometimes didn't.

Why was I, like so many kids, fascinated with these men? That's easy. They were heroes. How the fuck did I know? I just knew that these guys were on television. They were loved and adored by people and all they had to do was score a goal or make a great save. They didn't have to talk. They didn't have to learn. They were free. What could be better? No worries about school or jobs or parents or people. All you had to do was play hockey well. That's what I really wanted. I wanted love. I wanted attention. I don't think I gave a damn about playing for the Boston Bruins. This wasn't the world of Roch Carrier's story, *The Hockey Sweater*, this wasn't about me emulating Rocket Richard. I just wanted someone – anyone – to like me and pay some attention to me. Me me fucking me. If heroism meant that my parents would love me, then what the heck, I'd bite.

We were all chasing something that wasn't, isn't, and won't ever be. Too bad most of us – those who were fortunate – didn't recognize that until we were in our thirties and forties. Children learn through emulation and imitation, but eventually stumble off on their own paths. And hey, don't give me this nonsense about it being a predicament of modern society. As Homer's *Iliad*, witch burning, the Bible, and post-1950s Orson Welles have shown us, human history has always had its share of idiots. Today, there's just more of us.

We're not entirely foolish. The dirt of the hero constantly fascinates us because we know it's there. We've been in the slime ourselves. I was drawn to Doug Harvey because he drank, didn't fit in. In short, he seemed like a human being. His apparent faults made me respect him all the more. I didn't want to know how perfect these guys were, I wanted, maybe needed, to know how faulty, fucked up and human they were.

The NHL is like every other business. It's trying to sell you a personality, a feeling, something that will relieve the pain of your seemingly miserable and pointless existence.

Ironically, as the NHL has become more scientific in its business practices, its players have become as bland as a blank hockey puck. I grew up following Esposito, Lafleur,

Clarke, Chico Resch, Billy Smith, Tiger Williams, Dave "The Hammer" Schultz, Cournoyer and Dryden. Even though I was clouded by youth, these guys, even from the vantage point of a thirty-six year old, seem more authentic than today's players. They didn't seem as far removed from our own humdrum lives. Most of these guys came from small towns, from working-class families and grew up doing the same things the rest of us did. It's a bit of an illusion because our exposure to these players is always filtered through media. But even when you look back at some of those old TV interviews, there was still a hint of a personality in the player. "The players in Harvey's time always had something to say," says Red Fisher. "Today's players, starting with Gretzky, all sound like they belong to the same library and take out the same books. They all say the same damn thing."

Ah yes, Wayne Gretzky, the poster boy of bland. Gosh. Golly. Shucks. No personality. No dirt. Always smiling. No faults. The Barbie-doll wife. All filled to the roll-up-the-rim-to-win with small-town politeness: "Mr. Pocklington." "Mr. Bettman." "Mr. McNall." A robot, a perfect soundbite of a role model for a faceless, ad-drenched generation of intimacy-gapped spectators. Sundin, Lemieux, Kariya, Sakic, most of the roster of the Ottawa Senators: dull as a random thought. Everything that comes out of their sanitized droning mouths is rejected sitcom dialogue: "It's a team game... The boys played well in front of me... Personal achievements mean nothing unless the team wins... We've got to give it 110 percent tonight... We're really excited about this year's team." A carefully choreographed breath of nothings. "I hardly ever quote a player," adds Fisher, "because he sounds like the guy next to him and the guy playing his position in the twenty-nine other cities."

It's little wonder that the media chases after guys like Theoren Fleury, Tom Barrasso, Brett Hull, Jeremy Roenick or Gino Odjick. They're among the few players that openly display their emotions. They come off like guys who crap just like you, me, and my asparagus sandwich-making mom. In the pre-Gretzky era, there were no visits from team media advisors or public relations twits, no golden cliché handbook. Guys spoke from their hearts, very much in the heat of the moment. They came off raw, brilliant, courageous, embarrassing, stupid and funny. Perhaps no better example exists than the 1972 footage of Alan Eagleson giving the finger to the Russian crowd, or of a frustrated, exhausted and angry Phil Esposito blasting the entire country for booing Team Canada '72. Espo was rough and raw, but always real.

It's easy to understand the players' reluctance to say anything meaningful to the media. Quite often their words are taken out of context or just blatantly misquoted (although probably not as often as we're led to think). In fact, an honest, interesting player is so unique that whenever one is forthcoming, it becomes a major headline. Any time Brett Hull or Jeremy Roenick call the NHL a lousy product, the media lap it up. Or take an example: following two losses that cost the Vancouver Canucks first place at the end of the 2002-03 season, captain Markus Naslund said that his team "choked." At last, some honesty. But what happens? The media turns the word into such a big thingamaroo that

Naslund ends up being forced to back away from his words, blaming the heat of the moment and all such nonsense.

I wonder how Doug Harvey would have handled the media today. He might have done okay because he was picked on quite regularly during his early years with the Canadiens. Still, the media seemed to have a code back then. Their job was to report the games, not what the player did off the ice. While you might find a few covert references to Harvey's drinking, the media, for the most part, never mentioned Harvey's (or anyone else's) drinking antics. Besides, a lot of journalists sucked the bottle and probably got trashed with Harvey and other players, so they had to be pretty careful. It's a bit of a quandary: journalists are responsible for covering hockey, yet by playing a part in ignoring the surrounding realities of players' lives, they help to turn the players into walking cardboard caricatures.

It's ironic that the very things that guys like Lindsay and Harvey fought for have further alienated the player from the fan. Thanks, in part, to their roles in setting the table for the National Hockey League Players' Association in 1967, almost every player nowadays is a millionaire (the average salary in 2003–04 was $1.83 million). Players today are better educated. They've got a body of people around them to guide, protect and gouge them: family, lawyers, trainers and agents. In some ways the little boys have grown up, but only because – as is the case with Eric Lindros – they've got mom and dad on the payroll. Players are more like businessmen. It isn't a boy's game any more. It's a multimillion-dollar enterprise, and they want a share. Who can blame them? If owners are willing to throw money around, then so be it. I'd take the cheque too, and so would you.

The owners don't mind shelling out the extra money for players because they've found ways to increase revenue through the construction of bigger arenas with expensive corporate boxes, and assorted merchandising and television streams. Or they just jack up ticket prices. And while NHL attendance has been slipping of late (both Ottawa and New Jersey were short of capacity during playoff games), some folks don't seem to mind paying more.

The cheapest tickets for a 2004 Ottawa Senators game were $20–25. That gets you a seat near the roof in the Family Fun Zone ("family fun" means daddy has to stay sober). In the case of the Senators, you're going to pay $50 just for seats for you and your kid (aren't all NHL fans white, heterosexual breeders?), $10 for parking, and maybe another $20 for food and drink (assuming daddy DOES stay sober). $80 to sit at the back of the rink. I make a decent enough income but I sure as hell cannot afford to attend more than a couple of games per season. High prices, though, aren't new. Bruce Kidd and John MacFarlane note in their 1972 book, *The Death of Hockey*, tickets for the 1896 Stanley Cup game cost $12 (which translates to around $300 today). Why people want to pay these huge sums of money is baffling. Why not go to the casino?

As for the game itself, there are some differences from Harvey's time. The players didn't wear helmets and were smaller in stature. In general, the players were not as conditioned as today's robo-players like Gary Roberts. And with the size difference, there was more space on the ice to manoeuvre. Players actually skated with the puck and tried to stickhandle around the opponents rather than just shoot it in. But, overall, the differences are small. There was just as much stickwork, hooking, and clutching and grabbing then as there is now. In fact, King Clancy called Harvey "a magnificent cheat and the master of cling and clutch." These players were mean bastards. Everyone talks about the goals that the Rocket and Howe scored but these guys were dirty, angry, borderline head cases. Richard had problems controlling his temper and frequently lashed out at opponents, and, most famously, with a stick or a fist at referees. Even Harvey, the apparent Mr. Calm, had a pretty nasty temper that went back to his childhood.

As Milt Dunnell wrote, "Harvey breaks most of the bylaws in the book and beats the rap by looking like a deacon who has suffered a hot foot while singing in the choir." Harvey fought players and fans. In 1948, while playing for the Montreal Royals, Harvey punched a Valleyfield fan and broke his wrist. In 1956, he jumped into the stands after a Red Wings fan who had been heckling him all night. During a 1959 playoff game against Chicago, Harvey punched out a fan who was attacking referee Red Storey. He also injured players like Lindsay, Gaye Stewart and Fern Flaman with questionable hits. Unlike a lot of today's players, Harvey was rarely repentant. After almost spearing the life out of the Rangers' Red Sullivan, Harvey maintained that Sullivan deserved it for kicking Harvey's skates (one of those unwritten codes in hockey). Anyone who says today's game is more violent, unsophisticated or unsportsmanlike than the Original Six era (or even hockey of the seventies and early eighties) is misguided.

The NHL implanted the myth, but it was the media that nurtured, refined and adapted it. One of the great scams is the sports section of a newscast or paper. If you take away the real community activities like lawn bowling, ball hockey and high-school track meets, the rest of it is nothing more than free advertising for the business of professional sports. Every hockey summary, statistic and profile is one big free ad for the National Hockey League.

From a team and league perspective, the hockey media should be a pretty nifty deal, but it ain't. More than ever, media and public opinion are influencing a team's direction. Players, coaches and managers are all second guessed. Every trade, call-up, signing and cut is heavily scrutinized. The flurry of public opinion has created instant experts and the illusion that "anyone could do that job." And, if it means getting more bucks out of the fan, it appears some owners will insist on their managers taking heed of everyman's words.

The pinnacle of fan influence is the March trading deadline. It's a day that is more anticipated than the Stanley Cup final. Fans tune in to the radio, TV or internet weeks before the deadline to read about all the rumours. The NHL recognizes the publicity. It's a second wind of sorts, an opportunity to re-energize fans' excitement which can wane over the long season.

But let's give the commentators and fans some credit. Never before has such a high level of irrelevancy and meaninglessness been achieved with such extreme desperation and urgency. As Kierkegaard once suggested, people want freedom of speech in lieu of the freedom of thought they never use.

It's hockey heaven today. There are zillions of types of hockey cards, sticker books, radio shows, websites, newspapers, twenty-four-hour hockey channels, DVDs, hockey video games, and man, you can even buy almost any jersey from any time period. (Not only did I recently buy a retro Bruins jersey from '71-72, but after looking around Estonia for five years in search of an Estonian team jersey, I finally managed to track one down in 2002 only to discover that the damn thing was made in Canada!) And boy, check out the novelty items: keychains, t-shirts, mousepads, toy Zambonis, mini Stanley Cups, piggy banks, screen savers, hats, socks, underwear, blankets. And hey, even your toddler can get in on it. Pops can doll him (or her – it's a gal's game now too) up in a bib or PJs of the team of his (dad's) choice while feeding the kid with cute little team-logo-adorned forks and spoons out of team-logo-adorned baby cups and plates.

Even better, there's no more worrying about using Dad's old gas mask or Mom's Eaton's Catalogue for goalie equipment. Almost every sports store (yes, they have stores *just* for sports) now has affordable goalie masks, goalie pads, stronger nets and fancy sticks. There is NOTHING we cannot have today.

So why is it still not enough? How come that retro Bruins jersey didn't do anything for me? Am I chasing things that weren't there to begin with, in search of ghosts from a past that wasn't? Why do we want to possess more of something that isn't even there to begin with? It's become one big lie, a cinema that makes you think you're seeing and feeling something that isn't there, that makes you think you're unique and special when you're just like everybody else.

As I write this, I'm bouncing back and forth to the TV, watching the Ottawa Senators trying to avoid being eliminated in the 2003 conference finals. I'm sitting here demythologizing my relationship with hockey and yet my heart is pounding and I can't sit still as the game heads into overtime. Maybe I just want a little serendipity as I finish this – in part – eulogy to a life lived in Ottawa. But, in truth, this game is an anomaly. It used to be that *every* game drove me crazy with tension and anxiety. These days I don't feel the need to watch every game. Even during these 2003 playoffs, the interest is waning fast. In the middle of a close second-round game between the Flyers and Senators I actually left and went out to play ball hockey. Better to play than watch.

Maybe hockey isn't an escape from my home, my drinking or myself anymore. It's more like a side dish, like a bag of chips. Maybe that's why I felt nothing when I bought that old Bruins jersey or the Loblaws sticker book. I keep trying to buy emotions so I can turn them into something concrete and absolute, something I can feel in my hands. Isn't that what consumption is all about? Isn't that what advertising tries to sell us? Ads promise us the unreachable and non-existent. All this anger I feel towards those white-towel-waving idiots with Senators flags who spend their civil servant days calling in to sports radio shows is a projection of my own frustrations. Hockey was supposed to fill a gap, but I was asking it to be something it could never be.

The Senators score in overtime. I scream and jump, immediately decide to buy an overpriced ticket for game seven. I don't care. I've never attended an NHL playoff game and I want to feel that pre-game electricity. I want to absorb the atmosphere, to feel part of something. Of course I realize that I'm being a sucker. I'm blowing $130 for near-the-roof seats. I'm gonna drive thirty minutes to the arena and probably pay $15 to park. In a sense I don't care. It's just money. Sure, the egghead in me, the guy who just cannot shut up and enjoy it, calls me a sucker. Yeah, yeah, yeah, I know that I'd probably feel the same emotions if I just went to a bar and watched the game with friends. So what? This is a moment I want to lose myself in. I'm fully aware that it carries almost no meaning beyond that moment.

I just heard the Senators' team president on the radio saying that in most American cities, people only get excited just before the game and during it, whereas Canadians are eating, sleeping, dreaming hockey. He says this like it's a good thing. I dunno. The American way, for once, seems a tad healthier. That being said, I'm not going just for the game. I'm not sure I really care who wins, although, yes, it would be nice if Ottawa won. I just want to go out for a few hours, and feel a part of something, to get a little friendship, community and intimacy. It's like my ball hockey team, the Cyclones. I don't really care about the score. I'm just going out to be with friends, real friends, not the cardboard faces of my hockey cards.

Maybe it wasn't hockey that changed. Maybe we just grew up.

SAD MEMORIES
I CAN'T RECALL

"Oh demon alcohol / Sad memories I cannot recall"

—The Kinks, "Alcohol"

"Experiencing insobriety night after night is not the way mature men are supposed to behave."

—Dave "The Hammer" Schultz

The Rangers?
Jesus.
Fourteen years and this is what I get: the Rangers.
I hear they practice on a puddle above the rink.
Might as well send me to the minors.

Addiction bottles you with the impact of thunderous silence – a force so intense you are swallowed unawares. Existence reduced to extremes. You stagger between moments accompanied by tuneless instruments, every movement determined by invisible strings. Inevitably, you fall short. An evacuation of emotions collapses you into the hopelessness of a stained shirt. You reach an almost peaceful apathy, a mundane aftermath of despair. The echoes of memories are reduced to incomprehensible shadows. You can't see it, though you know it could not but be. A life atrophied. You were. You are not. Will you be?

A puck. A bottle. There really wasn't any difference. Harvey was addicted to both. Hockey destroyed Harvey's life as much as drinking did. Or did they? Were they escapes from responsibility and shyness or did they help him run from the darkness that swallowed him without warning – a darkness he acknowledged, but never understood?

Contrary to what some may believe, the pub was not an invention of the industrial society. At least as early as the sixteenth century, the pub, tavern or alehouse was the hub of village life. Not only was the pub a place of business and for socializing, it was also a centre for travel, accommodation and various sporting activities, such as horse racing, stick fighting, lawn bowling, cockfighting and casual ball games.

With the rise of the industrial city, there was more leisure time. Pubs became an important retreat for men, providing a venue for bonding and a refuge from familial and work obligations. Men could talk about their work experiences, laugh, sing and just enjoy one another's company. The pub was a forum for shared release. To this day, the function of the pub remains largely intact. However, since the emergence of television, the pub has become reconnected with sports. Pubs not only sponsor and support recreational and professional local teams but they've also become meeting places for both athletes and fans.

Up until the 1940s, alcohol abuse was treated primarily as a sin, a social evil that turned respectable men into drunken brutes. The word "alcoholic" first appeared in public discourse in a 1943 *New York Times* article. Now the drunk was no longer an evil, immoral wild-man but simply a sick soul who used drink as an escape from alienation, anxiety, depression and the various pressures of the modern world.

In June 1961, the Canadiens traded Harvey to the New York Rangers. In return they received rugged defenceman Lou Fontinato.

Ken Reardon (who became assistant general manager of the Canadiens after he retired as a player) and Frank Selke were sick of Harvey's "antics": the contract games, his association with Lindsay's players' "union," the jokes, the drinks and the attitude. In their minds, Harvey was a spoiled little boy.

"As a player," says Reardon, "Harvey was excellent, but if you're talking about personalities and things like that, he was different from the others. If we were told that we were going to go on a train and wear a shirt and tie, he's not going to do it. He didn't give hell for authority. It was very aggravating because as an official for that team he could really embarrass you in front of the rest of the players. 'Where's your shirt and tie?' 'Oh, I didn't feel like it today,' he'd say. And you weren't really gonna open up a can of worms and have a big fight with the guy.

"He hated all this publicity, but I said to him, 'Why do you do things that create publicity?' If you don't like the booing, do the things that everybody else does. But he didn't seem to want to be one of the mob. One time he missed the train and he had a friend who owned a private plane and gave lessons. He phoned the guy and chartered his own plane. When we got to the hotel in New York he was sitting there."

Harvey might have been management's nightmare, but Reardon knew the fans worshipped him. By making a deal to ensure that Harvey became a player/head coach with the Rangers, Reardon and Selke made it look like they were doing ol' Doug a favour. Helping him make that transition from player to coach was all so virtuous. They knew that Harvey couldn't coach. Sure he knew the game well, but how could a man with no self-discipline be expected to discipline others? It was a cruel joke on both Harvey and the Rangers. Despite saying that he "vaguely" remembered the Harvey trade, Reardon's account is fairly clear and concise:

> "How'd you like to get Doug Harvey?" Reardon asked Ranger Manager Muzz Patrick.
>
> "Is there any chance to get Doug Harvey? Are you serious?"
>
> "Sure I am ... but there's a bit of a catch to it."
>
> "What's that?"
>
> "You've got to make him the coach."
>
> "Sure, I'll do that. I don't mind doing that as long as I get him."

Reardon continues: "I wanted the deal to look like he was being assisted to a better plan. It went over very well. I didn't get too much hell. Very little as a matter of fact.

"This was not a fair deal ... but it was better than a fair deal because we got rid of him. Fontinato was a blunderin' bust. I couldn't justify it on that level, but we weren't sure when Harvey was gonna turn it on or off near the end. Harvey was a pain in the ass like you wouldn't believe. I told Muzz Patrick that I'd take anybody. But I wasn't giving Muzz Patrick and the New York Rangers a bouquet of flowers."

"That son of a bitch," says one former Hab and friend of Harvey's. "[Reardon] married the boss's daughter [Reardon's wife was the daughter of Habs owner Donat Raymond]. Reardon didn't think much of me and I didn't think much of him. He was jealous of Doug. Doug should have stayed with our team right to the end of his career. Rocket did, Beliveau did. Doug was not a coach."

Alcohol arrives an angel, but leaves a demon. Once that first drop hits the brain, all doubt vanishes. Life is never simpler. You can do this, that, and the other thing. Nothing can stop you from being who you want to be. No one is going to stand in your fucking way. Your head is light. Thoughts are high. Clarity has never been closer. Time stops. Hate, past and present, fades with each sip, and as sip turns to gulp. Cravings, perversions and longings that lay restlessly within daydreams now come gusting along as sweet sounds piercing the staggering winds. Light turns to darkness.

Blackout.

After the storm, the winds calm. Memories unrecalled. Bruises. Pain. Headaches. Whispers. Shits. Pukes. Misery. Voices, from where? It was supposed to cure the demons and deliver the sunken soaked soul from the miseries of abandonment into a wonderful nightmare of loquacious delusions. This is gone now. There is no deliverance. Your timeless underwater oblivion was as miserable as the dry one above. Life returns as a drifting blur of insomnia-inspired fragments.

●

Jesus that's a lot of money.
How hard can it be to coach?
Maybe I can do it.
I could be a coach, general manager. A whole new career.
I'll show those twin fucks.

In the late spring of 1961, Harvey signed a three-year deal worth $27,500 per year to be player/coach of the New York Rangers.

"At first there was a little apprehension because there weren't playing coaches in those days at all," says former Ranger defenceman Harry Howell, "but we soon found out in a hurry that he was an excellent coach and could have been an excellent coach for a long time."

Perhaps hoping to stick it to Reardon and Selke, while recognizing that this trade was – whatever its intentions – a good opportunity for a thirty-seven year old on the downside of his career, Harvey showed up in the best shape of his career. "That particular year he was all business," says Howell. "Our practices were crisp and fresh, far different than what we had for some time in the past. He was still a very good hockey player and he played extremely well but he also added a lot of new twists to the Ranger offence and defence."

Harvey also earned the player's respect because he treated them like men. "I'm not going to knock on doors and baby guys," Harvey said during the Rangers' 1961 training camp. "They know my rules and I expect them to keep them."

"He could lay it on the line if things weren't going by his standards," remembers Howell, "which were high standards. He would get very upset, but not very often – most of the time he was very even keel. He wasn't used to missing the playoffs or struggling to make the playoffs but we were a lot better team with him."

I had my first real drink (as opposed to the vodka shots not-really-my-pops gave me at age six) at fourteen. A group of us *Ottawa Citizen* paperboys had won a contest to see the Montreal Expos play. We snuck into some older kids' rooms and took a few cans of beer. There were, I think, four of us sharing a room. Fragments. One kid was out of his fucking mind. He was throwing chairs out the window and pissing on the bed. There was little sleep. That kid, and maybe another, got banned from the game and probably fired from his paper route.

At the time I was still playing football and soccer, but the lure waned compared to that of friends, girls, my dick and booze. Every weekend we drank. If we were lucky, we found a guy's place to guzzle and get silly at. If not, we found bushes, alleys and even a stairwell in the local mall. Man it was fun. I remember feeling real giddy all the time. I didn't care what people thought of me. I could just let go and live and enjoy. The girls were prettier. Hell, the girls were *possible*. More than that, my confidence grew. I had dreams now. I'd be a football player, a rock star. Sure, these were pretty normal dreams for a sober teen, but in my sobriety I had very few dreams. Not-really-my-pops had become fully ingrained in the macho, brow-beating rage of Cop Land. I wasn't a son; I was a suspect. While he was always reminding me what a no-good shit I was, my pal booze was telling me otherwise.

I wish I'd enjoyed alcohol more. Like sex, it was such a blind, groping, perverted lust. It was just another hole. But what the hey, isn't that the life of all post-pre-pubes?

●

They just wanna make the playoffs here.
That was never enough in Montreal.

The Rangers were a lousy organization and a lousier team. They hadn't made the playoffs in three seasons and hadn't won a Stanley Cup since 1940. Their arena was the smallest in the league and most days the team was forced to practice on an abnormal figure skating rink that had aluminum boards. And unlike Montreal, hockey was not even close to being the most popular sport in town. For a man who had spent his entire life in the same neighbourhood, New York would be a major adjustment.

That being said, there were some bright spots on the Rangers roster. Andy Bathgate and Dean Prentice led the way up front while Harry Howell (and now Harvey) gave the Rangers a decent back end. In goal was the one and only Gump Worsley. The Rangers also had some talented young players like Jean Ratelle, Vic Hadfield and Rod Gilbert on the horizon. In fact, things started out for Harvey and the Rangers and by mid-season, they were in third place. Harvey was playing thirty minutes a game, nominated to the all-star team, on his way to his seventh Norris Trophy... and coaching. The players seemed happier with Harvey than their previous coach Phil Watson, who was – to put it mildly – not a player's coach.

"He doesn't yell at you," said Gump Worsley at the time. "He explains things in a quiet voice and the guys like that."

"He treats us like pros," said Andy Bathgate. "Nobody ever treated us like that before. It's a different feeling."

"I think that just by watching Harvey play you learn a lot

and we talked about the game a lot," said Howell in 2003 (he won the Norris Trophy in 1966–67). "He knew hockey about as well as anyone I ever played with. He was a scholar of the game and we talked and talked and discussed different situations. I'd been in the league for eleven years when he came in and I picked up a lot of tips just watching him out there. Certainly didn't hurt me at all."

Harvey's inspiration began to wear off by the end of the 1961 and by December, the Rangers were in the midst of a major slump that saw them fall to fifth place in the six-team league.

As hard as Harvey tried, the Rangers were no Flying Frenchmen.

Even by sixteen, I was freaked by my drinking and went to a guidance counsellor. Perhaps I just wanted someone to pay attention. Being an alcoholic gave me a name, made me a somebody. Maybe the invisible woman and not-really-my-pops would notice me. They didn't. They were too busy getting divorced (a heavenly day I tells ya). Pretty soon not-really-my-pops, sports and high school were all gone. And the invisible woman finally revealed herself. It wasn't pretty. She was a madwoman: lonely, angry and compulsive. She left notes all over the house, made threatening phone calls to not-really-my-pops, who'd shacked up with some blonde, and even sent dead flowers to the new couple (that was sort of cool in a that's-ballsy-but-I-wouldn't-do-that sorta way). Beyond that, I just continued jumping into those holes. Pretty soon there was a new hole. I'd forget what I did the night before.

From my twenties to early thirties, my drinking just got worse. Ironically, this was the time when my, umm, professional life was getting itself together. I landed a job I never should have had. I drank, drank and drank. I'd wake up beside strangers in places I didn't recognize. For about six years my life dissolved into a blur of fights, fucks, blackouts. It was all one big blackout. The worst one (I think) involved being knocked unconscious, coming to, and then immediately discovering that I couldn't walk. I'd broken my ankle. That last thing I remember is leaving a bar, getting in line for fries, calling a woman who pushed past me a bitch, and wrestling with the guy accompanying her. Must have hit my head on the way down. A taxi driver helped me to his cab and drove me home. My wife was so angry she just helped me to bed and dumped a bag of frozen peas on my ankle. Stayed in the hospital for three days, roomed with two guys who drank their way in too. During my recovery I stayed sober, went to AA meetings, watched the Leafs beat the Senators in six, and vowed never to drink again. By month's end I was in Los Angeles on business, and getting drunk daily.

Player/coach?
I don't wanna coach.
I don't wanna leave Montreal.
And I don't wanna be a blue.

And you know what? Fuck all those anti-hero sentiments and all those books and stories and movies that turn the addict into some sort of tragic hero. There was nothing heroic or romantic about any of this. It was all pretty dumb.

I'm a player but I can't hang out with the fellas. I'm so sick and tired of going back to that hotel by myself.
Drinking alone isn't any fun.
Where's Gump? He's always got a bottle handy.
Where's Ursula?

As early as March 1962, Harvey began expressing doubts about returning as a coach: "I don't know what I'm going to do. I probably won't know until I get back to Montreal in the spring and have a little time to think about it."

The pressures were clearly starting to get to Harvey. He lived an hour away from Madison Square Garden in Long Beach so that his family could join him. "It's been a big change for me," said Harvey. "There are lots of things to consider. It's been hard this year. I don't feel as peppy as I used to. It's even hard to get 'up' for some of the big games."

Harvey's coaching predecessor Phil Watson then came out and smacked Harvey in the press: "Harvey doesn't know what he's talking about. Harvey can't put his team through a hard workout because his tongue would be hanging out."

Ross Hutchings, a close friend of Harvey's, remembers a time when the Rangers were playing in Montreal: "When he came in with New York one time I met him at a restaurant and a lady came up and asked for his autograph. He makes a nice note for her and after she goes, he takes a picture out of him in his New York uniform and he says, 'Ross, I still can't picture myself in that god-darned uniform.' It broke his heart to go there."

Two things saved me, and both of them read like cheap plot twists hardly worthy of a Douglas Sirk film. First, there was my son. His conception saved me. It was that simple. I could keep being angry with my parents, and my life, or I could fix the fucking thing and be a father to this boy. Slowly... and I mean slowly... the drinking binges were less frequent.

My son was like a ghost. In him, I also saw this miserable little boy that still raged inside me. Here was my chance to stop all this shit. If I could love my son, I'd also be saving that other messed-up boy.

We're in the playoffs.
I knew I could do this.
They love me.
I bet I could run for office.

Then came the hockey game. It was winter. I was driving home from the liquor store. I had an article to write (yeah... ha ha ha... writer and booze... what a cliché). That meant spending the night in the basement, getting drunk, staring at a computer screen, and eventually doing some writing. On the way home I noticed a hockey rink. I saw the lights, the blurred figures gliding around. In one bizarre moment I suddenly wondered why I wasn't out there. I think I cried... maybe not... I'm not sure. I went home, wrote whatever article, and got drunk. It was the last time I took a drink.

I won't do this anymore.
I miss drinking with the boys.
I just wanna hang out with the boys.
I don't want to coach. Too much responsibility.
Just let me play the game.

Doug Harvey wasn't the only hockey player. He wasn't the only alcoholic. He wasn't even the only hockey player who was an alcoholic. But he was the best.

Harvey drank as a junior but he really learned how to drink in the Navy. Drinking was a man's game. That's what *real* men did. And the more you drank, the more you were a man.

Military officials didn't mind the drinking. If it was gonna give the boys that extra dose of bravery and fearlessness, what the hell. Booze was also the great ice breaker. It enabled the men to feel more at ease with one another. But it was all hollow bluster; these boys drank out of fear, anxiety and loneliness. Alcohol made war a little more meaningful and dying a little less meaningless.

When the Second World War ended, Harvey went from one male world to another: the Montreal Canadiens. There wasn't all that much difference. Both were sanctuaries of masculinity. Men. Masculinity. Manly. Machismo. What a crock of shit. If these men were the pillars of indomitable masculinity, why were they drinking in the first place? Sure, it was a partial release from whatever perceived tensions they had in their domestic and work lives. But, for others, it was the electric shock that jumpstarted their lives. Whether the problem was intimacy, fear, or self-confidence, drinking temporarily patched over the cracks. Ironically, drinking turned these he-men of men into slurring slobs. They hugged each other and spouted niceties.

Hockey was a high-pressure job. One screw-up and that could be it (Detroit manager Jack Adams used to carry around one-way train tickets to the minor leagues in his pocket). They drank to forget the fighting, the mistakes and the humiliation. A player could be sent to the minors or outright released for the slightest transgression, which included injury. So a lot of players endured enormous pain just to avoid losing their spot on the team. "You don't think I'm gonna take any chances on being out of the lineup?" Harvey told columnist

Milt Dunnell in 1956. "If I'm out of the lineup and lose my skating legs, you know what these guys will say about me next year. They'll say: 'Poor Harvey… he just doesn't have it anymore. That's not for me.'"

As Dave "Tiger" Williams wrote in his autobiography: "It seemed to me that a lot of guys were just plain scared, scared of fighting, scared of making mistakes and looking bad. And maybe that was the explanation for all the drinking. Or perhaps it was the cause of it." Whether worried about injury, error or demotion, drinking soothed the nerves.

Players also had a lot of leisure time between practices and games (more so in the Original Six era than today), so the local bar became a gathering point where they could talk about plays or bitch about coaches and management. As with other working men, drinking, for players, was not only a bonding experience but also a reward for hard work or victory, or a consolation.

"When I first got to Montreal," says Dickie Moore, "I didn't drink and I didn't want to drink because my dad had drunk and I said, 'No, I'm not gonna start,' but after a few seasons someone told me, 'If you're gonna stay in this league, you better drink.' But I didn't want to drink. After the game I'd go to the store and have a sandwich and a coke and I was happy with it."

"The schedule for a lot of guys," writes Tiger Williams, "was to go to the morning practice, then slide off to a bar until four or five o'clock before going home for some supper and a long sleep. I told the guys there was too much drinking… it didn't make me popular."

I want friends, not employees.
Who am I to tell them what to do?
Who am I to say you're not good enough for this team?
Let someone else worry about it.
I just wanna play.
I just wanna drink with the boys.

"Everybody drank beer in those days," says *Montreal Gazette* journalist Red Fisher. "Everybody still does. This is what they grow up on, on their way to the NHL. They drink beer as juniors and they certainly drink beer at the NHL level. Some drink more than others and Doug was in the group."

Players like Tom Johnson and Jean Beliveau acknowledge that Harvey drank more than others. But back then no one was too concerned. Harvey was a fun-loving guy who always showed up ready to play. So he had a few more beers than everyone else. He earned them.

"It was after the game that Doug drank," says Jean Beliveau. "We knew because we travelled on the trains or went out after games. But he played well. And if an athlete is doing his job well, then it doesn't matter so much if you don't agree with the way an athlete lives."

Fuck it. I quit.

After the Rangers were eliminated by Toronto in the 1961 playoffs, Harvey returned to Montreal. One night he paid Red Fisher a surprise visit: "At about 1 am," remembers Fisher, "my doorbell rang and there's Doug Harvey. I said, 'What are you doing here? Do you know what time it is?' He said, 'I just wanted to tell you that I'm quitting as coach.' I invited him and we argued for the next four hours. 'How could you quit as coach?' I asked him. 'You took the team to the playoffs. They have signs in Madison Square Garden saying *We Love You Doug*. You can't quit as coach. 'I wanna be with the boys,' he said. I told him that if he coached a few more years, he'd likely become general manager. But with Doug, if you said black, he said white. So after four hours of debate, I didn't even come close to convincing him. It's ridiculous, but that was Doug Harvey. That was part of his character, but that doesn't mean it was right."

"When Doug did quit the coaching job at the draft in Montreal, he went up to see Muzz Patrick," says Harry Howell. "I assumed Muzz was going to offer him a pretty good contract because Doug was the toast of New York. He could have had anything he wanted because he was so popular, but he went up to Muzz and said, 'I want to be one of the boys. I don't want to coach, I just wanna be a player.' It's as simple as that. I thought he made a terrible mistake because he was an excellent coach and would have made an excellent coach in the long term and he just walked away from it when he was thirty-seven years old. I didn't understand it at all. He could have gotten anything he wanted: a three-year contract, a five-year contract ..."

"Maybe we were consuming too much," recalls former Canadien defenceman Tom Johnson, "but nobody thought about it. It was about companionship and friendship. Doug liked to have a good time and he thought a good time was drinking with his buddies."

Train rides.
Bridge games.
Beers.
No-practice clause.
The boys.
Life is good.

In September 1962, it was announced that Harvey would return to the Rangers strictly as a player for the 1962–63 season. It was a sweet deal. He was reportedly paid $30,000 (a raise of about $2,500), making him the highest-paid player in league history. And not only would Harvey not have to coach, he would also be allowed to skip practices so that he could return to Montreal and visit with his family periodically.

Throughout his career, Harvey had tried to find a career outside of hockey. At various times he was a carpenter, had an aluminum siding business, ran a sports equipment shop with his brothers, and even owned the Doug Harvey Hockey School (which ran from 1961–79). In the early 1960s, he went in on a restaurant called Chez Harvey. By 1962, things were starting to go sour with the business and Harvey missed a number of practices early in the season so that he could return to Montreal and address the problems.

"He had a bad partner," remembers Ross Hutchings. "Apparently when the restaurant closed up at 2 am, he'd put his hand in the till and take a bunch of cash and go out on the town. He wasn't a good fella." Eventually, the partner fled town with all the money. Hutchings, an accountant, was approached to have a look at the restaurant's books. "In nine months," says Hutchings, "Harvey lost about $65,000."

●

Thank god for Gump.
He likes a party.
Knows how to enjoy life.
Always gotta bottle around.

As a coach, Harvey had been good about his drinking, but when he returned as a player, his old habits returned. "I heard from the players he was living with that he was back to his old ways again," says Harry Howell. "In two months, he made up for what he had missed the year before."

The relationship between hockey and alcohol extends beyond the players. Not long ago, I could sit back with a case of beer (probably with some NHL-related gift inside) watching Hockey Night in Canada live from the Molson Centre. In the 1980s, Molson Brewery owned the Habs (and twenty percent of the Maple Leafs) and sponsored Molson Hockey Night in Canada, while Carling O'Keefe Breweries owned and sponsored Nordiques telecasts. In fact, original Black Hawks owner Arthur Wirtz, a major liquor jockey, used hockey and boxing to sell beer.

Why are they booing?
Just like the old days.
Ignorant sheep.
Now I'm too old and slow.
They don't want me anymore.

Skipping practices not only pissed off his teammates, but it didn't help his conditioning. Harvey was inconsistent for the first half of the 1962–63 season and Rangers fans were soon chanting, "Harvey must go." He turned his play around by mid-season, but his glory days were clearly behind him.

Wanna send me to the minors.
Screw them. What do they know?
They don't know hockey here.
Let them release me. Someone else will call.

In July 1963, the Rangers left Harvey unprotected. He wasn't impressed, but the Rangers clearly had no use for a thirty-eight-year-old player on the downside of his career – especially after Harvey had made it clear that he didn't want to coach or manage.

When Harvey missed most of the Rangers' 1963–64 training camp, the Rangers had reached the end of the line. On November 26, 1963, the Rangers gave him his unconditional release.

Harvey figured he'd catch on with another team, but despite early rumours that he might go to Toronto or even back to Montreal, no NHL team wanted him. Within days, a desperate-sounding Harvey said that he wasn't "above playing for nothing for a few weeks to prove" that he could still play.

No one called.

This is a relationship that extends well beyond the confines of the NHL. Men's recreational hockey leagues, for example, are often referred to as "beer leagues." In these leagues, socializing during and after the games is more important than the games themselves. In fact, local bars and restaurants, eager to attract heavy-drinking customers, sponsor many of these teams. The bar will sometimes pay the cost of the team jerseys and offer a discount on beer. In the ball hockey league that I played in, not only did the league add a bar and patio to its facility (an old airplane hangar) but it actually encourages drinking by putting a portion of money that a team spends on beer towards their entrance fee for the next season.

If there were any doubts about the complex and often problematic relationship between alcohol and hockey, a short-lived 2004 season ticket campaign by the Tampa Bay Lightning surely put them to rest. During game one of the Eastern Conference playoff series between Lightning and the Philadelphia Flyers, the St. Pete Times Forum scoreboard advertised that anyone who paid $100 towards 2004–05 season tickets would be eligible for unlimited free beer during the remainder of the playoffs.

The response garnered so much outrage that the Lightning eventually stopped the offer, but the fact that the Lightning employed this marketing tactic clearly shows just how entwined alcohol (notably beer) and hockey are. It was as if the Lightning had finally just come out and played the cards that everyone knew they had: "Look, you buy some tickets, we'll get you drunk because we know that's just as important to you as the game itself."

The game has become an amusement park of sorts flooded with a variety of loud distractions, give-aways, movie trailers, contests to ensure even if the game itself is sub-par the fan still has a good time. And naturally, there's nothing like four or five beers to enhance the illusion. Beer drinking and hockey have become synonymous for both player and fan. Another modern-day myth rewritten as truth.

Doug Harvey was not an alcoholic anomaly. Terry Sawchuk, Tim Horton, Harvey Jackson, Johnny Quinty, Murph Chamberlain, Dick Duff, Bob Probert, Bryan Fogarty, Darren McCarty, John Kordic, Ken Daneyko, Chris Simon, Petr Klima, Derek Sanderson, Reggie Leach, Paul Holmgren, Pelle Lindbergh, Craig MacTavish, Steve Chiasson, Jere Karalahti and Theoren Fleury are just a few of the players who've battled the bottle. Most of these, though, are well-known examples. The trail of minor-league alcoholism is vast and silent.

Given the prevalence of alcohol and alcoholism in hockey, it's astonishing that, until 1996, the NHL, unlike other professional sports, had no substance abuse policy. Under the policy, players can voluntarily participate without penalty. Previously, players were suspended automatically for alcohol or drug use, but each team was left to police their respective environments. This was problematic because hockey is a fraternity. Many players become coaches, then general managers, and a couple even owners. In short, many of those who are now in managerial roles know alcohol as an intimate part of hockey. Are they able to step back and see the extent of the problem?

Of course, given the intimate relationship between hockey and breweries, does the NHL even want to take a good hard look at the problem? It's not exactly in its best interests to slow the flow of beer when your major sponsors are breweries. Besides, the NHL is always conscious of image – especially in the USA – and to even acknowledge a possible problem would potentially create the image that the NHL is a sport of drunks. (To be fair, the troublesome relationship between alcohol and hockey is not isolated to the NHL and North America. Finland, Russian, Ukraine, Slovakia and the Czech Republic have all had their history of booze-related problems.)

Even with the existence of the policy, there remain questions about its effectiveness. Rumours abound about players who've faked their urine tests and Theoren Fleury – who continues to battle drugs and alcohol – called the policy "an absolute joke" on national television. That being said, friends and family and support groups can only do so much for an alcoholic. If he doesn't want to hear, then absolutely nothing that anyone says to him is going to make a difference. So Fleury can complain all he wants about the effectiveness of the NHL's policy, but clearly he is also a man who doesn't *want* to quit drinking. Until he does, any and all substance programmes will remain ineffective.

It shouldn't be all that surprising that the relationship between players and alcohol doesn't end after the final whistle either. A number of players have wisely – or unwisely – invested in restaurants and taverns (including Harvey, Gretzky, Toe Blake, Don Cherry, Yvon Lambert, Henri Richard, Brad Marsh and many others) after their careers were over. These businesses allow the player to take advantage of the marketing value of their name, secure themselves a stable post-NHL career, and keep them close to fans, players and the game.

●

Am I slowing down?
I don't feel any different.
Sure the body ain't what it was, but this game is mostly mental.
I know that better than most of these kids.

●

Many friends and teammates believe that Harvey's drinking got worse after his trade to the Rangers. This isn't quite true. First of all, there were times when Harvey's drinking was pretty bad with the Canadiens. But he was young and his body could tolerate the abuse. Secondly, Harvey actually appears to have drunk significantly less during his first year coaching the Rangers.

But as Harvey continued to drink, his body (like any other drinker's) most certainly became increasingly tolerant. Early on, he'd be satisfied with a six-pack, but years later, he'd barely be abuzz from a two-four and moved onto hard liquor. At the same time, alcohol and hockey had been a successful team. They appeared to rid Harvey of those dark moments. But during the 1960s, Harvey found the darkness was increasing. Alcohol is a fuel for depression. Sure, it suckers you initially so you can take on the whole fucking world for a few hours. But, the next day, those little demons are back and stronger with each visit. Soon, you're drinking just to keep them away.

By his last year with the Canadiens, booze was starting to slow Harvey's game down. He was reaching his mid-thirties. Natural talents are of little use if you're huffing and puffing. Hockey was slipping away from Harvey. He may not have shown it, but he was scared. He tried to find business success outside of hockey but he couldn't do it. His drinking and depression got in the way of the decision-making process. In 1962, right around the time he quit coaching the Rangers (a poor business decision itself), Harvey got screwed out of thousands of dollars with Chez Harvey.

When Harvey's drinking seemed to suddenly worsen after he resigned as Rangers coach, it wasn't due to a broken heart. Harvey must have been scared. He lost his restaurant and failed as a coach. He was very quickly realizing that hockey would not always be there. And with those demons coming steadily and more frequently, the frustrated Harvey drank the same way a two-year-old has a tantrum. Drinking helped him flee from the adult world. He was midway through his life and only now was he beginning to see that he was still just a boy.

Why didn't anyone help him during his playing days? Some players didn't notice, others didn't feel it was their place. By the time his heavy drinking was noticeable, Harvey was a respected veteran on the Canadiens. It would not be proper for young guys to approach "the great Doug Harvey" about his drinking. Some really didn't even notice how bad it was. "I don't know about his teammates," notes Red Fisher, "but as a newspaper guy and a friend I never knew how much he drank until he stopped playing and then everyone noticed how much he drank. I had no idea how much this guy could put away. I learned that he was doing a lot of it while he was playing and yet I can't say enough about him as a player."

Worse still, there were many who had no sympathy for Harvey. They saw alcoholism as a weakness and couldn't understand why Harvey wouldn't just stop drinking. This attitude pissed off Dickie Moore: "Doug shouldn't have been drinking when he was playing, but some old-timer was crucifying him. I told the player 'This is a time when you help a guy, you don't shit on him.' He said, 'Well, you had to see him.' I said, 'That's not Doug Harvey, the booze is doing it, not him.' If they knock Doug, I'll stand up for him."

I quit drinking two years ago. Saying it hasn't been easy is stating the obvious. Surprisingly, it's not the alcohol that I miss. What I really struggled with was how to fill up all this sober space and time I now had. That was a real bitch. I think I figured out that I'd gained about half a day. I managed okay. I wrote more and started exercising. I took up ice hockey, boxing, and even ran a marathon; in fact, I think exercise has just become a new addiction.

Then there were the social occasions. No more buzzes to soothe me through a reception. But the absolute toughest part of sobriety was coming to terms with the reality that I've spent my life not really being myself. I let the alcohol define my personality.

So here I am, all of a sudden, wide awake inside this body and mind that I don't fully recognize, let alone comprehend. Even worse, everyone around me had, naturally, pigeonholed me as this other person. So, all at once, you're trying to figure out just who it is you really are while attempting to convince others that you are not this person you always told them you were. Almost makes you wanna drink.

Who needs the NHL?
I started at the bottom; I'll finish at the bottom.
What do I care?
The way up is the same damn way back down.

●

Was drinking the same for Harvey? It's difficult to say because he didn't stop drinking until the last three or four years of his life. I dunno. You dunno. No one knows but him and he's dead now.

●

For the rest of the 1960s, Harvey would play the part of Odysseus, roaming hockey's wastelands in search of home and himself.

AM, AM NOT

I've got nobody to talk to, nowhere to go. This is no way to live.

—Doug Harvey during his Rangers days

Just as the river where I step is not the same, and is, so I am as I am not.

—Heraclitus (fragment 81)

What do you do when you can no longer be who you thought you were?

Hockey gave Harvey plenty of warning that it was done with him. The trade to the Rangers was the first sign, yet he remained faithful throughout the 1960s – playing briefly with Detroit, St. Louis and a handful of minor league teams – before his options ran out. He could be a stubborn man. He didn't listen to others, and worst of all, he didn't listen to himself. Or maybe he just didn't like what he heard. Perhaps his deep-seated fear of *what might be* overshadowed the truth of what he heard: he was finished as a hockey player.

Most players have left the game in their early to mid-thirties. Either their bodies outright refused to cooperate anymore or they simply grew up and realized that it was time to get on with life. The mid-thirties is that crossroad for many people, that time when they finally begin to *get* life, to understand who they are and what they want from life – a time when you begin to recognize the fragility of the whole damn ride.

Some ex-teammates and friends love to romanticize this period in Harvey's life: he loved the game so much he'd have played for free; he didn't care about the money, he just wanted to play. A load of nonsense, all of it. Certainly Harvey languished in the minor leagues during the mid-1960s out of passion, but it was arguably more to be around "the boys" than it was to play the game. He also needed the money. With a variety of failed business ventures and his own apathy towards finances, money was always welcomed. If hockey's still paying, why stop playing?

Harvey's body started to go by the end of his tenure with the Canadiens, but he managed to outlast most because of his smarts. He'd always known how to conserve energy through proper pacing and positioning. His hockey mind was sharp enough to manipulate the ice, freeing up energy for his increasingly weary and bloated figure. It was a good balance. But drinking destroyed that. He tired faster; his mind fell a step behind. His hockey instincts weren't enough to compensate for the damage he was doing to himself. If he hadn't been drinking, he probably could have played even longer. In footage of him playing with Detroit and St. Louis, he's overweight, bloated, and seems lost on the ice. In some rare 1967 film footage of Harvey in Detroit, he's just skating around and around, going nowhere. Just like his life.

Fortunately for him, there was expansion.

The six-team NHL doubled to twelve in 1967. The new

teams included the Los Angeles Kings, Pittsburgh Penguins, Oakland Seals, Minnesota North Stars, Philadelphia Flyers and the St. Louis Blues. Expansion meant more jobs. More jobs meant the boys could keep pretending to be boys for a few more seasons.

Harvey landed a player/coach job with the St. Louis farm team in Kansas. During the 1967–68 playoffs, the Blues called Harvey up to help the team. He went, played well defensively, and helped the team reach the finals, where it lost to the Canadiens. Harvey stayed with the Blues the next season, 1968–69, but prior to the start of the playoffs his career came to a bizarre and abrupt end. There were a few tales about what happened. One friend, Joe Gorman, suggested that Harvey took a lead pipe to the head from two men who'd previously scuffled with him. Another rumour had Harvey's teammates Barclay and Bob Plager taking the lead pipe to his head. The truth, as Harvey biographer William Brown discovered, turned out to be stranger. Turns out that Harvey and teammate Barclay Plager were out on the town. After changing his mind about calling it a night, Harvey turned to get back inside Plager's car. Plager already had the car in reverse as Harvey opened the door, which knocked him to the ground. The result was a fractured skull and a sad end to an NHL career.

Friends and family knew that Harvey had a drinking problem. But they didn't, and couldn't, see that there was more. Alcohol fuels depression, making it difficult to separate booze blues from manic depression.

When your grief is out of sync with the cause, you're suffering from depression. It's one thing to go apeshit after someone you know dies, quite another to do so when a computer downloads too slowly. Those with manic depression (bipolar disorder) are a tad more extreme. Just as they have these periods of disproportionate grief, they also have soaring, superfluous highs that often manifest themselves in, let's say, shopping sprees.

Again, I don't know whether my mom is manic or not, but when she was down, she'd rush out and spend money she didn't have on things she didn't need, like a fucking rowing machine, a stationary bicycle or collector's plates. Buying stuff gave her a buzz, but after a few days, the high would wear off and the purchases were forgotten, left to collect dust and cat fur in our pussy-piss-stenched basement. Life with manic depression means a non-stop dance (unless you're medicated) with suicidal despair and unwarranted euphoria.

We've reached a stage in our society where depression is taken more seriously – it's no longer written off as a case of the blues. However, I wonder if we're eliciting manic tendencies ourselves by taking it so damn seriously now. The slightest darkness or greyness is plucked out, put under the microscope and medicated. You're no longer just shy now, you suffer from social anxiety. There's a pill for that. I'm not raging against medication, but we seem to have lost sight of the essence of human nature.

Heraclitus suggested that human nature is a cycle of

conflict. Perhaps depression and its attendant doubt, despair and paranoia are normal counterparts to the happiness, calm and confidence that we also seek. And think about the world we live in. Over the last century we've been living in a society that is constantly telling us that something is wrong with us, that unless we buy such-and-such product, we'll remain unhappy and unfulfilled. Who the hell wouldn't be consistently depressed by the images and sounds of failure blasting our senses every minute of our apparently empty lives?

Virtually every player that I spoke with who knew Harvey said they didn't notice a thread of depression in him. That doesn't mean anything really, or does it? Were his frequent displays of apparent rebellion just Doug being his own man (as most friends claim) or were they a release of whatever darkness he was enduring?

Then there was the drinking. Alcoholism comes with its own built-in depression. The booze initially takes you to false heights before dropping you like a wet sandbag. In fact, Harvey didn't even know he suffered from depression until he was diagnosed in his sixties.

Did he ever wanna kill, ever wanna just grab someone by the throat and squeeze out the juice of life, or maybe wind up and pound with the throttling shrug of a jackhammer? Was he possessed of an anger so impending that it caused anxiety in the stomach and tightness in the shoulders?

You simply want to hurt, to bring pain, to do something…
to anyone – anything to excavate and eradicate that chaotic
whirligig running amok in your head. You just want to get rid
of that pain. Nothing but time can cure you.

Never do you feel more alone, more imprisoned in your
body. You want nothing more than to escape yourself.
Sometimes you're pushed to self-inflicted pain. You lie in bed
and kick madly at air. Your head shakes violently from side
to side but you stop short of banging it into the bookshelf.
Instead, you unleash a fury of punches on your pillow because
you know that this is all a fucking joke and that you're not so
far gone as to destroy yourself so heroically.

There is no lonelier moment. You can't connect with
anyone; you can't bear to be with yourself. Then it just fades.
Sometimes, you manage to fight the short-circuit in your
head and sleep. Most times, you get drunk. If you're lucky,
the booze will carry you to tranquility.

But that's if you're lucky. Sometimes, it's like throwing a
match into a room of fireworks. All self-control vanishes. You
lash out incoherently at everyone. You go out there looking
for it, waiting for the slight twitch of an eye, the tone of a
voice, maybe the FUCKER who didn't signal before changing
lanes. You will find a fault, and when you do you, explode
into a rage against whatever unfortunate stranger is there.

On the oh-so-rare occasions you talk, you tell someone what
you're feeling and almost instantly the clouds part, the sun

beams, the knotted bubble pops, the storm in your head passes. You've no idea what even caused the storm. What the hell could have made you so twisted?

During the 1970s, Harvey remained in the spotlight for mostly unflattering reasons. In 1971, he ran for political office in Montreal representing NDG. Money and the surprising admission that his hockey career was finished were Harvey's primary motivations for running: "Well, hell, I'm too old to play now ... and let's face it, I can use the money. At first I thought council paid only $5000, but it's more like $7000."

But it wasn't entirely about money. In a telling speech, Harvey spoke of wanting to create a place for the senior citizens of NDG to gather, but it almost reads as if he were referring to his own existence: "You know, I often see those old fellows, pensioners and that, just sitting around in the parks with nothing to do, and nowhere to go. Hell, everyone needs somewhere to go."

It didn't matter. Harvey was resoundingly defeated in the election 19,377 votes to 5,189.

A few days after the election, Harvey was arrested at Ottawa's Uplands Airport for carrying a handgun. Harvey and friends had been out drinking and eating Chinese food. They returned to the empty airport around 4:30 am to fly back to Montreal. Harvey, clearly a little sauced, began performing handstands for on-duty RCMP officers. They approached the men and asked to inspect their bags. Inside Harvey's briefcase, the officers found a loaded revolver. Harvey later claimed that he was carrying the gun to protect himself after being assaulted during his election campaign. The charges were eventually dismissed.

In 1972, the Hockey Hall of Fame refused to accept Harvey in his first year of eligibility. It's hard to believe that Harvey, the man who redefined the defence position, failed to make the Hall of Fame in his first year of eligibility. He figured it was the booze: "They won't put me in because I'm not averse to sampling the nectar of the gods now and then." He paused to take a sip from his gin and tomato juice (surely, there were better combinations available) before continuing: "The difference is that I'll hoist a few in full view of everyone where some other guys will sneak around the corner to do theirs. I am my own man."

Maybe he was right. Maybe it was the booze. Stick-up-his-ass Selke was on the voters' committee. He told Harvey that if he wanted to get in, "You've got to help me." What did that mean? Did that mean Harvey had to stop being himself? They'd fucked people over before (1930s star Busher Jackson, who also drank, wasn't elected until 1971), but maybe Harvey just needed an excuse, needed to be a martyr, needed a reason to keep drinking. Here was a player who didn't know where he was going from one day to the next. Perhaps the Fame folks were hesitant because Harvey might lace up the skates for the new World Hockey Association (WHA). How embarrassing would that be: to induct a Hall of Fame member only to have him come out of retirement with a rival league?

It was all hot air in the end. A year later, Harvey was unanimously inducted, but he went fishing instead of attending the ceremony. However, about ten years later, at the urging of Canadiens President Ron Corey, Harvey went to the Hall to finally accept his induction.

Reporter: "How do you rank yourself among defencemen?"

Harvey: "I don't know. I've never seen myself play."

In early 1973, Harvey accepted a job scouting for the Houston Aeros of the WHA. Harvey had a decent eye for talent and was apparently the key man responsible for luring Gordie Howe and his sons, Mark and Marty, to Houston – a move that, following the Winnipeg Jets' multi-million-dollar signing of former Black Hawk star Bobby Hull, further solidified the WHA as a serious rival to the NHL. But Harvey was disorganized and never kept thorough files. Perhaps he took the job out of desperation; not only did he need money, but he needed the rink. Harvey's son, Doug Jr., told one writer that his father was gone as much after hockey as he was during hockey.

When Harvey was at home, no one knew what to expect of the man. Would he be drunk? Would he be angry? Would he even come home? He clearly loved his wife and kids. He had an extraordinary capacity for others, but love, family and intimacy came in brief, unexpected spurts, then vanished. The drinking, the depression (unrecognized still) made him restless. He was always somewhere else.

They had always said he was free, that he did what he wanted, that he was true to himself. Then they said he was manic-depressive. Does that mean if he was "normal" he wouldn't have been himself?

Did he speak softly to corral his demons? The ice provided Harvey with a refuge before booze came along. He didn't have to speak or even think. Hockey was a game of instinct. You acted. You flowed with the guidance of your body. The ice was an antidepressant.

Was he the scared little boy who feigned coolness but secretly wanted to be loved and accepted?

Intimacy was always a problem – unless Harvey and I were drunk. Intimacy requires trust, a willingness to let people see the pus, warts and shit. It means coming to terms with humiliation and recognizing that weakness is not the domain of pussies, faggots and girly girls. That means you have to trust people. To trust people you've got to trust yourself. To trust yourself means needing confidence in yourself. To have confidence in yourself means knowing yourself.

The only time my parents touched me was to smack, kick or punch me. They never uttered *any* expressions of love. It wasn't a Micky Ward–Arturo Gatti slugfest. Mostly, it was the waving of fists or flicks across the side of the head. No, most of their damage was verbal. I was steadily reminded from about the ages of five to eighteen that I was a no-good-shit, stupid idiot. Those were the good days. At least they noticed me. Most of the time, I was just ignored. My confidence never left the building because it had never even entered it.

I see this lack of confidence in most of my extended family. There's always this little wall between us when we speak. Rarely is there eye contact. Talk is sprinkled with sarcasm. The strange thing is I can tell that they all want to reach out, that they all want to love and be loved. They're all pretty normal people, but it's almost as if there's this loose wire that just needs to be soldered.

Intimacy was a stranger to Harvey, too. Sure, he could laugh it up with the boys and with children, but there was a wall when it really counted.

Maybe it was a gender problem, too. Why were men able to be so loose and free with their pals but deceptive, mischievous little shits with their wives and girlfriends, the very people who were supposed to be their best friends? Could it be a fundamental flaw with marriage and its all-or-nothing ultimatum, that pressure to be all things to each other?

Drink made all that fear of intimacy go away. Why do you think drunks all hug, kiss and slobber over each other so much? Drinking is sometimes nothing more than a means to release frustrated intimacy. Sometimes the feeling is overwhelming; if it's kept bottled up for long enough, that discharge is hard, fast and occasionally violent. Like Cinderella, we try to absorb every goddamn beautiful feeling of this drunken moment before it turns back to a lifeless stone-faced pumpkin. Because of the almost manic desperation to connect, everything blurs. It's a Dionysian shindig. We sleep with strange women, hug men, punch strangers, dance like tornadoes, puke out guts, and then black out. We do whatever we feel like. No processing, just being, doing, living.

Prior to a game against the New York Islanders in 1974, the Montreal Canadiens honoured their Hall of Famers. Harvey showed up half-corked in a denim outfit. As he walked out onto the ice, he slid – surfer style – on the ice. Instead of joining his teammates at centre, Harvey he went directly to the benches of the current teams and struck up conversations with a couple of the players. The crowd's roared greeting quickly turned silent. Harvey eventually made his way to centre ice, but there was a feeling of embarrassment and awkwardness in the air. The next day, legend has it, Islander players saw Harvey at the airport wearing the same denim outfit.

It was a strange night, but one that showed the conservatism of the public. Some truck that ol' anti-hero nonsense about Harvey being his own man, being a rebel. What a pile of sheep dung. Harvey was a shy man. He didn't like public events. To ease his fear, he drank. He turned the moment into something more playful and comfortable. Did it really reveal just how fucked-up Doug Harvey was or was it a case of revealing just how crassly dull and predictable the masses could be? Why was this moment embarrassing? I'd find it *inspiring* to see someone break from the usually staid, half-assed pre-game ceremonies. Regardless, it was another event that fuelled the nasty rumours about Harvey's state of mind. The Canadiens washed their hands of him. It would be another ten years before he was on Forum ice.

By 1978, Harvey's scouting days were done, done and done. He was living in NDG taverns now. He called one, the Antonine Tavern, his "office." He'd come full circle: beyond the alcoholism, which was reaching point-of-no-return levels, the bars were his last link to hockey. The practices, games, players and trains were all gone now, but the tavern remained. In "the office," the booze and the boozers made Doug Harvey real again. This was the game now. He was still a star here, the hockey player hangin' with the boys.

Harvey had a lot of friends, but most of them had settled down with families and moved on to second careers. They didn't have the time nor the desire to drink every night so, as they faded to the sidelines, Harvey found new friends in the tavern.

Ah yes, the age-old question: why didn't someone help him? Where were his friends, family and colleagues? They all *tried* to help him, but talking to an addict is like trying to explain sex to a four year old. Harvey was already a stubborn SOB. *No one* was gonna tell him to change. Instead, Harvey became more defiant: "Sure I could stop if I wanted to, but I don't." He became increasingly vocal and boastful about his drinking: "When they drop this body into the ground, it won't rot for a long time. It's full of alcool. It's got its own embalming fluid."

The "office" became his sanctuary from silence. Here he was simply Doug Harvey, the great Canadien! People flocked to him. They wanted to hear stories. They wanted to hear what the Rocket was really like, or about the time he almost killed Red Sullivan, or how he felt after he "scored" the Stanley Cup winning overtime goal in 1954 after tipping a Detroit Red Wings shot past his own goalie, Gerry McNeil (who was so devastated that he retired from hockey for a year). They wanted to know what he thought of hockey today. No one bothered him about his drinking in the office. All those demons vanished, their voices of doubt silenced.

He was rarely sober then. The binges became longer and more frequent. He hardly knew where he was any more. The family, for the most part, was gone. Ursula had booted him out. She'd endured his shit for decades: the unpaid bills, the late-night stumbling, his disappearance for days, even weeks. She was done with it. No Doug was better than this Doug.

The "office" became a home.

In 1983, Harvey's old pal Joe Gorman heard that he was having a rough time and offered him a job at his racetrack, Connaught, in Aylmer, Quebec (five minutes from Ottawa). Harvey worked as a security guard, carpenter and handyman. Behind the racetrack stood a luxurious train car once used by Canadian Prime Minister John Diefenbaker for cross-country campaigns. Despite some wiring and lighting problems (which Harvey fixed), it was a snazzy, furnished abode. Harvey moved in. When he wasn't working at the track, Harvey either went hunting, spent time with his new girlfriend, Lorraine Armour—who occasionally came down from Montreal for a visit – or just stayed in the car alone.

Harvey's life didn't turn around overnight in Aylmer. He continued his habit of not drinking for weeks or months and then, without warning, disappearing for weeks. One night he stole the racetrack's ambulance for a joyride. Another night, the Gormans had to collect Harvey from an Ottawa jail after an incident at a local bar. But in general, the Gorman family provided stability, comfort and privacy. He spent a lot of time with the family and frequently babysat their young children. In a sense, Harvey was returning to his childhood. The Gormans, despite being about Harvey's age, became surrogate parents to the sixty-year-old man. In fact, according to William Brown, Harvey even called Gorman's wife, Pilar, "Mum."

It would be a load of cow chew to say that Harvey rediscovered himself in Aylmer, but he clearly benefited from having more time to himself. He was away from the pressures of media, family and friends. The railway car became a new sanctuary for Harvey. In the car, he had privacy – a space where, finally, no one could tell him what or who he was supposed to be.

In 1984, things started to go a bit better. Harvey was featured on a TV segment called *Legends of the Game*, hosted by Bobby Orr. Then, in 1984, Montreal fans voted him to the Canadiens' all-time all-star team. A year later, in September 1985, the Canadiens announced that they would finally be retiring Harvey's number two.

Not long after the ceremony, Joe Gorman bumped into Canadiens President Ronald Corey at the Ottawa airport. Gorman told Corey how well Harvey had been doing and suggested that Corey hire him as a player scout for the Ottawa–Hull area. In December 1985, Harvey was officially welcomed back as a part-time scout. He was given a car and a $30,000 salary.

Not long after Harvey rejoined the Canadiens, he moved back to Montreal to live with Lorraine.

While his drinking slowed, his stomach swelled. He was tired all the time – so tired he couldn't even play golf. He refused to see a doctor. Bravado? Not likely. Some say that Harvey had quietly endured all sorts of injuries during his hockey days and this was no different. Bull – he was scared. He knew something was wrong and, like many people, he didn't want to have a doctor confirm his fears. If you don't know it's comin', there's nothing to fear.

But finally it was too much. In late 1988, he went to the doctor. His liver was shot. Cirrhosis. He'd have to go to the hospital.

Harvey spent the last eleven months of his life in the Montreal General Hospital. He died on December 26, 1989. Boxing Day. You can only fuck with the body for so long.

Dickie Moore loves to repeat a heroic line from Harvey's final days. A few weeks before he died, Harvey apparently told Moore that he wouldn't change a day of his life. He had no regrets. But what else was he going to say? Harvey did what he wanted to do and succeeded beyond what many others accomplished. He became among the best. He wasn't a great husband or father, but he wasn't that terrible either. His kids have grown up and understand him a bit better, and appear to still love him deeply. And for every Ken Reardon or Frank Selke, there were dozens of people who loved Doug Harvey.

What does it mean to live a good or bad life? Good and bad are just categories we've created, nothing more. As someone, somewhere said, we create our own meaning. Maybe a bad life means a life unlived, but what does it mean to live? "Know thyself," said a wise Greek. But to know thyself, one must find oneself. To find oneself, one must search. To search is to live. To live is to know thyself.

Even his friends (except for Rip Riopelle, who says he always felt there was something unknown about Doug, like he had his own private room somewhere), teammates and associates all speak as if they knew with certainty who Doug Harvey was. Maybe they think they did, but for the most part they just repeat the same worn clichés. While reading Brown's Harvey biography, I was struck by how often I read the same quotes that I'd heard directly and indirectly from players and friends. That's not unusual, but what got me was how the words said nothing. They were all vague generalizations about Harvey's on-ice skills and rebellious, freewheeling behaviour. A faulty memory is certainly a factor when you consider that most of these guys are now between seventy and eighty years old. Still, there's something missing. It's almost as if the players have reconstructed the past based, not on their memories, but on what they've heard or read over the years. It's almost as if second-hand reports have made them doubt what they saw or heard or felt. The past has become a tidy little package of linear coherence played out by living hockey cards. Everything we need to know is on the back.

But life isn't that way, isn't that ordered and predictable.

I never spoke to Harvey's family. I don't blame them for not wanting to talk to me. There's been so much darkness associated with their father. They just want to get on with their lives. But I wonder if they even really knew him. There's a prevailing belief that a family knows its own more than anyone else does, but I don't for a minute believe that. We all wear masks. We all have private rooms. It's true that at times others see in us what we don't see ourselves, but even that insight is fleeting. I doubt Harvey's family even knew who he was.

We never really know anyone. That's obvious. We think we know some people inside and out, only to discover that we know very little. I guess most of what we project to people is an illusion or a dreamworld to begin with. We all wear masks, even those of us who think we act openly and honestly. We generally choose what we want others to see. Conversely, we also define those around us. The person we see is, in many ways, a projection of ourselves. We create the other person.

●

But maybe Pilar Sancho, Joe Gorman's ex-wife, was right when she told William Brown, "He had no desire to conquer his demons, because Doug had no demons. Doug was Doug and he accepted himself the way he was. And there was never a question about whether he drank too much or not. He didn't think about it. It was part of him just like being green-eyed was part of him."

Maybe Doug Harvey just *got it.* Maybe he unconsciously understood life better than most of us and saw the absurdity (in a ha-ha, non-woe-is-me manner) of the whole damn thing. He lived a life that life deserved. He ran rampant through it… doing, trying, being… wading through layers of encrusted horseshit and recognizing the hollowness of societal compartments, labels and rules. Let others toe the line in hockey. Let them forsake their identities for fear of losing their jobs, their money. Harvey said, "Fuck it." No one was going to tell him who he was going to be. In that sense, there is something heroic about Douglas Norman Harvey. We're living in a world that is hell-bent on effacing individuality, on uniting us all like drones through a generic, friendly, unprovocative culture. Screw Gordie Howe and Wayne Gretzky. Harvey was not gonna stop living just to please Frank Selke and Clarence Campbell. He wasn't gonna stay at home and be a proper pops just cause that's what you were supposed to do. He wasn't gonna work some crap job just to make ends meet. He was gonna play life like he played hockey – at his own pace. If you want the puck, come and fuckin' take it from me.

Harvey never made it easy for himself, or anyone else, for that matter, but he didn't just lipsynch his way through life. He stumbled, skulked and even fell straight on his ass. Maybe manic depression was a blessing that kept him from being stagnant, from taking easy roads. Sure, he lacked the easygoing diplomacy of a Gretzky or Jean Beliveau, but that's what was so fascinating about Harvey. He wasn't like all those other cardboard figures of celebrity. Gretzky and Beliveau are like the woman I think my granny is: clean, inoffensive and predictable. They don't like to ruffle feathers. They want to get along with everyone. Harvey couldn't embrace that mask. It wasn't that he didn't care about other people; he just didn't know how to please them without sacrificing his own integrity and truth. He also knew that to seek wholesale approval was a load of pixie dust.

I remember an artist telling me that he'd "found his room in the house of art." It all sounded so damn warm, heartfelt and fuzzy, and what a crock. Why would anyone want to stay in the same room his entire life? Why cut yourself off from the possibilities? Why make such a drastic final choice while you still have the option of making choices? It's the old Odysseus dilemma: should I stay or should I go? Harvey surely recognized this when he was coaching the Rangers. Yes, there was a degree of immaturity at play: he was not a disciplined person; he was scared of coaching. Coaching and managing was no different than selling cars, sporting goods or aluminum fucking siding.

I turned thirty-seven today. I'm about the age Harvey was when he was traded from the Canadiens, when his life began a bit of a downward spiral. I'm near the end of this thing and I still wonder why why why I needed to write this book and why Doug Harvey was so seemingly essential to it. I never met the man. I never saw the man play. I never saw the man drink. Why not Ted Lindsay (whom I planned to write about as early as 1997) or Busher Jackson?

I've been sober for more than four years now. I've hardly spoken to my mother in that the same period of time. Oddly enough, I've sort of reconnected with not-really-my-pops after a ten-year silence. In between, I even found and met my real father. Turns out he doesn't even know who his father is and isn't interested in becoming mine. Heh heh. So hurray for me... the circle is closed, fait accompli. All along, I saw this book as a eulogy to a bitter past. Harvey's life was supposed to lead me back to my own past so that I could forgive those who shrouded it in darkness, including myself.

What a stupid fuck I was.

Here I am trying to create balance around me, trying to show that the world is a cycle of emotions and thoughts, that nothing is absolute, that nothing is either/or. All the while, I fooled myself into thinking that this book would help me close a door. Certainly, I think I've got a better understanding of what went on. I grew up in a world of deluded extremes. Life at home felt so muted, violent and dark that I embraced whatever would take me away from that. Hockey was the first light. It let me think I was somewhere else, someone else. But I never let go and only now realize that I was embracing the shadows of things, not the things themselves. Like Plato's cave dwellers, I was living in darkness, seeing only the outlines of the world. Alcohol took over when hockey wasn't enough. I gave up hockey cards for bottle collecting. For almost thirty-six years I was a silhouette, a hockey card.

Like for all kids, my world was one of absolutes, an either/ or one in which my parents ruled. Now that I'm a parent, I can look back upon them with a more balanced gaze. They were just a couple of young, confused people who met at the wrong time, under the wrong circumstances, and made a succession of selfish and stupid decisions. In a way, the hate I feel is more towards myself than towards them. However bad they were, there were worse parents in the world. And anyway, I managed; it's not like they were out to intentionally harm anyone. The real problem is I can't forgive myself for being unable to forgive them.

I wanted to find the humanity, not the hockey card, within Doug Harvey, my parents, and myself. Whether I'm ready or not, I know it's time to put away the hockey cards.

Only now do I know what Doug Harvey meant to me. He not only unwittingly showed me how being human sometimes meant being covered in puke, warts, pus and shit, but that this was okay, that it was normal. Doug Harvey was never just a great hockey player or a down-and-out drunk. He was just a guy. He was born. He died. In between, he did a bit of this and a bit of that. He was strung together with the rest of us on a page of a book, trying to write his own verse before the page turned.

Acknowledgements

Aside from a ton of newspaper and magazine articles, I first must acknowledge Michael Ulmer's book *Canadiens Captains*. His very frank yet balanced chapter on Harvey led me here. Secondly, do yourself a favour and check out William Brown's biography, *Doug: The Doug Harvey Story*. It's an ideal factual complement to my impressionistic musings. Mark Anthony Jarman's *Salvage King, Ya!* and Bill Gaston's *The Good Body* are two of the best hockey novels out there.

I'd also like to thank the following people for their time: Roy MacSkimming, Howard "Rip" Riopelle, Joe Gorman, Chuck Rayner (who died just months after I spoke with him), Billy Reay, Red Sullivan, Harry Howell, Tom Johnson, Jean Beliveau, Butch Bouchard, Red Storey, Ken Reardon, Brian McFarlane, Ted Lindsay and especially Dick Irvin, Dickie Moore and Red Fisher.

Closer to home, I'd like to thank Dennis Sabourin, Tom McSorley, Barry Doyle, Signe Baumane, Michèle Cournoyer, Lauren Donen and my boxing coach, Chris Weissbach.

David Ehrlich is a remarkable friend and colleague who pushed me to finish. Without his support, I'm not entirely sure I would have managed to get off my ass and see this thing through to the end.

Richard Meltzer, Matthew Firth and Mark Jarman took the time to provide me with feedback on the manuscript. They are all fine writers and I'm flattered as all heck that they were so generous with their time.

I hope my mother and not-really-my-pops will understand. If not, so be it.

I have to thank my hockey mates from the Cyclones. They've all helped me, whether they realize it or not, finally find real pleasure in hockey.

Mark Jarman kept reminding me that all it takes is one to believe. He was right. And that one is Silas White. Wow, what can I say other than thanks for believing and taking a chance on this dark little story.

To my loving family: Kelly, Jarvis and Betty Neall. They were first-hand witnesses to those dark years and yet managed to have faith in me.

And, finally, to Doug Harvey, whose life and death led me down a strange new road.